NO NONSENSE GARDENING GUIDE™

FLOWERING HOUSEPLANTS

By the Editors of Garden Way Publishing

Longmeadow Press

FLOWERING HOUSEPLANTS

Copyright © 1990 by Storey Communications, Inc.

Material for this book has been adapted from *Keep Your Gift Plants Thriving* by Karen and Jim Solit (Garden Way Publishing). Used by permission.

Published by Longmeadow Press, 201 High Ridge Road, Stamford, Connecticut 06904. No part of this book may be reproduced or used in any form or by any means, electronic or mechanical, including photocopying, recording, or by an information storage and retrieval system, without permission in writing from the publisher.

No Nonsense Gardening Guide is a trademark controlled by Longmeadow Press.

ISBN: 0-681-40962-2

Printed in the United States of America

0 9 8 7 6 5 4 3 2 1

Prepared for Longmeadow Press by Storey Communications, Inc.

President: M. John Storey
Executive VP, Administration: Martha M. Storey
Publisher: Thomas Woll
Series Editor: Benjamin Watson

Cover and inside design by Leslie Morris Noyes
Edited by Sarah Magee
Production by Carol Jessop, Joan Genova, Judy Eliason, and Nancy Lamb
Illustrations by Elayne Sears

The name Garden Way Publishing is licensed to Storey Communications, Inc, by Garden Way, Inc.

Cover photograph © Don Johnston: Photo/Nats

Contents

THE NO NONSENSE LIBRARY

NO NONSENSE GARDENING GUIDES

Flowering Houseplants
The Successful Vegetable Garden
Using Annuals & Perennials
Landscaping for Beauty
Herbs the Year Round
The Weekend Gardener

OTHER NO NONSENSE GUIDES

Car Guides
Career Guides
Cooking Guides
Financial Guides
Health Guides
Legal Guides
Parenting Guides
Photography Guides
Real Estate Guides
Study Guides
Success Guides
Wine Guides

CHAPTER 1

THE WORLD OF FLOWERING HOUSEPLANTS

Winter, spring, summer, or fall, a dazzling array of flowering houseplants is available at florists, garden centers, and even supermarkets. Once you know what to look for, the most difficult thing about buying a plant is choosing among the many beautiful varieties available in every season of the year.

After you get your flowering houseplant home, you'll want to keep it flowering for as long as possible. Once the first bloom has faded, you can get even more enjoyment — not to mention a tremendous sense of accomplishment — by carrying your plant over to bloom again and again. With care and knowledge, you can have lovely flowering plants in your home throughout the year . . . and from year to year.

Showing you how is what this book is all about.

For each of the many magnificent plants discussed, this book provides detailed information on cultural requirements (light, water, fertilizer, repotting, etc.), both during and after bloom.

The following are some general guidelines.

SELECTING HEALTHY PLANTS

When choosing flowering houseplants, look for those with many buds, or a combination of blooms and buds. Although specimens in the fullest bloom may be the most immediately attractive, you want a plant that will be in bloom the longest after you take it home. That means choosing one with unopened buds.

Foliage should be green and unwilted. Yellowed, brown, or spotted foliage could indicate the presence of disease or pests. While wilted foliage could mean only that the plant has not been watered, it could also indicate disease. Avoid these specimens.

Also look for bushy growth. Long, spindly stalks can indicate the plant was grown with inadequate light.

PROVIDING IDEAL GROWING CONDITIONS

The single most frequently heard complaint about flowering houseplants is that they won't bloom again once the initial flowers have faded. The reason is almost always the same: failure to provide for the plant's cultural requirements. Most flowering houseplants are natives of places with far different climates from that found in most homes. To bloom again, each has its own unique environmental needs. For example, many of the plants available in winter require cool nights to thrive. They will not bloom again in a home that is too hot for them.

Inadequate or improper light, too much or too little water, the wrong fertilizer, or pots that are too large or too small are some of the other causes of failure to bloom.

The good news is that, when flowering houseplants are given the right cultural conditions, their initial bloom can be prolonged, and most can be carried over to give years of enjoyment and pleasure to their owners.

Many of the plants discussed need higher humidity than the average home provides. For most, this requirement can be met by use of a pebble tray. Many garden-supply stores sell bags of pebbles and clear plastic trays for this purpose, although any flat, shallow receptacle is fine. Just remember to keep water in the tray, but not so deep as to touch the bottom of the pots. Pots sitting in water can quickly cause roots to rot and plants to die.

Using a spray bottle to mist plants is not a very good substitute for a pebble tray. The mist dries quickly, whereas the pebble tray, from which water evaporates at a continuous rate, provides an even source of needed humidity. Also, with some plants, such as African violets, there is a risk that water sprayed on foliage can cause leaf spot.

Plant Care After Bloom

To get a flowering houseplant to bloom again, it must be treated properly after its initial glory fades. For some plants, such as fuchsia, this may mean a radical cutting back of the foliage and a period of time in a cold, dark place. Amaryllis foliage must be allowed to die back naturally. African violets, on the other hand, have virtually the same cultural requirements in bloom or out of bloom. You'll find specific guidelines on how to care for your plant after the blooms fade in the chapters that follow.

Many flowering houseplants do not require fertilizing until after the blooms fade. Then, proper food is essential for healthy growth and new bloom.

Different plants need fertilizers with different chemical compositions. Three numbers appear on the label of water-soluble chemical fertilizers. The three numbers, such as 15-30-

15, indicate the percentages of nitrogen, phosphorus, and potassium contained in the fertilizer, in that order. These numbers are used throughout this book.

REPOTTING

In general, flowering houseplants need repotting when water runs more quickly through the soil than it did in the past, when roots can be seen growing through the drainage holes in the bottom of the container, when the soil dries much more quickly than usual, or when there has been a lot of new growth since the plant was last repotted.

Most plants should be moved to a container no more than 1 to 1½ inches larger in diameter than the previous pot. Never use a pot that lacks a drainage hole in the bottom. If you don't like the look of pots, you can buy attractive baskets or ceramic containers into which the pots can be inserted. Just remember not to let water stand in the bottom of any receptacle in which your potted plant sits.

Different kinds of plants need different soil mixtures. The right soil mixture is given in the discussion of repotting for each of the plants in this book.

MOVING PLANTS OUTDOORS

Many flowering houseplants benefit from being moved outdoors in the warmer months. Some, such as Easter lilies or garden mums, are ideally suited to become permanent additions to the outdoor garden.

When putting plants outdoors, the part of the country in which you live makes a big difference. Throughout this book, reference is made to the zones from the United States Department of Agriculture's plant hardiness zone map, in which the country is divided into ten zones. The lower the number, the cooler the zone. The map is included for reference on page 8.

Planting Zone Map

Approximate Range of Average Annual Mimimum Temperature for Each Zone

ZONE 1	BELOW -50°F
ZONE 2	-50° TO -40°
ZONE 3	-40° TO -30°
ZONE 4	-30° TO -20°
ZONE 5	-20° TO -10°
ZONE 6	-10° TO 0°
ZONE 7	0° TO 10°
ZONE 8	10° TO 20°
ZONE 9	20° TO 30°
ZONE 10	30° TO 40°

Courtesy United States Department of Agriculture

WINTER PLANTS

AFRICAN VIOLET

No flowering houseplant provides a more splendid display of color and grace for so many months with such a minimum of effort as African violets. If you consider African violets passé or too common for your collection, look and think again. Their handsome foliage, symmetrically arranged in a flattened rosette, makes the perfect backdrop for delicate blooms which poke up between the leaves to form a bouquet in the center of the plant. Alone or in groups, these beauties always get a second glance and admiring comment.

DESCRIPTION

African violet hybrids are classified in many ways, including by size. Most of the specimens available for sale and found in people's homes are called standards. They are ordinarily purchased and displayed with an 8- to 14-inch diameter. However, plant shows often feature standards well over 2 feet across with leaves as symmetrical as the spokes on the wheel of an English racer. Many of the standards sold in plant shops have the potential to reach such size and perfection with less effort than people imagine.

AFRICAN VIOLET

There are also smaller African violets, known as miniatures, which do not attain a diameter of more than 6 inches and produce proportionately smaller blossoms. "Minis" are charming when planted in brandy snifters or terrariums. There are also trailing violets, which are lovely in hanging baskets.

Flower colors include white as well as shades of purple, violet, lavender, wine, pink, and rose. The flowers may be "single" or "double." The blossoms may be streaked, rayed, or edged with a contrasting color. There are many types of African violet foliage.

Violets are further classified into groups known as *series*. A series includes varieties that a particular grower claims have special and superior characteristics. The Optimara, Rhapsodie, and Ballet are three examples of popular and widely available series. Violets are frequently, though not always, labeled with both the series and the hybrid name.

The hardest thing about selecting an African violet is identifying a well-grown symmetrical specimen. To be symmetrical the plant must bear a flattened rosette of leaves arranged like the spokes of a wheel and not have produced multiple crowns or offsets (plants growing from the base of the mother plant, creating a helter-skelter pattern of foliage and flowers). Though most African violets will eventually produce offsets, you do not want your plant to start out this way, or its symmetry may be destroyed forever.

Look also for a specimen with flower stalks bearing several buds — an indication of a free-flowering habit. The leaves of your plant should be horizontal, not stretched upward, a sign that the plant has been grown in too little light. In addition, African violet leaves should not hug the container, a condition that suggests poor watering practices or exposure to lower than optimum temperatures. Avoid plants with a long bare stalk at the base, which suggests that numerous outer leaves have died and been removed. Finally, keep an eye out for mealybugs, a pest with an affinity for African violets.

Cultural Requirements

A properly grown African violet blooms several times each year in exchange for minimal care.

Light: The most beautiful African violets are grown under fluorescent lights. A standard-sized fixture, 4 feet long, equipped with two 40-watt tubes — one cool white and one warm white — fits the bill perfectly. The fixture and tubes can be hung in any reasonably well-ventilated room where night temperatures do not drop below 58° F. Space under a kitchen cabinet or beneath a book shelf will do beautifully. The light should be kept on 12 hours a day. Plants should be placed 6 to 12 inches beneath the tubes.

If an African violet is kept several feet from ceiling fluorescent lights, its leaves will stretch upward and the plant will fare poorly. However, directly under a fluorescent desk lamp, an African violet or two should do just fine, if 12 hours of light is provided and other cultural requirements are accounted for.

Don't be discouraged if you do not own a fluorescent light fixture. A window that gets the morning sun but is protected from the hot afternoon rays (which may cause foliage burn during summer) will do fine. Fluorescent light is ideal, but natural light is adequate.

Temperature: African violets grow best where night temperatures are 58° to 68° F. and day temperatures are 5 to 10 degrees higher. Plants should not be moved suddenly to a cool growing area. Instead, they should be adjusted slowly to temperatures below 65° F. Cold drafts must be avoided.

Moisture: African violets should be watered thoroughly when the top layer of soil feels clearly dry to the touch. Plants kept too wet may rot at the soil line; those kept too dry will wilt, lack vigor, and bloom poorly. Try not to pour water on the foliage, where it often accumulates in tiny puddles. If this accidentally occurs, simply tilt the plant slightly and shake off the water. With many fuzzy-leaved plants like African violets, water tends to cause spots on the foliage, especially on specimens placed in cooler growing areas.

African violets prefer a more humid environment than most homes provide, and plants benefit greatly from the use of a pebble tray. They also seem to do particularly well in groups, where moisture from soil surfaces evaporates after watering to humidify the air surrounding all the plants.

Fertilizer: Fertilize early every month with a water-soluble, chemical fertilizer, following package directions. Then apply fish emulsion around the middle of every *other* month. These two steps generally cause plants to grow quickly, bloom freely, and receive rave reviews.

Placement in the Home: If grown under natural light, African violets should be placed within a few feet of the window. Keep leaves from touching cold windowpanes and avoid drafty areas. Small groups arranged on glass shelves in front of a window make for a beautiful display. Glass does not overpower these delicate plants and provides an open, airy feeling.

Fluorescent light fixtures for growing African violets can be placed wherever the temperature range is suitable. When plants bloom, you can take them out from beneath the lights and move them to a coffee table or wherever they look best. Just remember to return them to the growing area within 4 or 5 days, for about a week.

Potting and Soil: African violets grow better and bloom more freely in smaller pots than other plants of equal size. For example, a 4-inch pot is suitable for a plant measuring 12 to 16 inches across. Just keep in mind that the soil in small containers tends to dry out fairly quickly, and plants require more frequent watering than those in larger pots. The shallow plastic pots often referred to as "bulb pans" are better than deeper containers for African violets because the soil in the bottom does not stay wet too long.

Plants purchased in 3-inch pots should be moved to 4-inch containers after they have made substantial growth, when the water runs through the soil more quickly, and when the soil dries more rapidly between waterings. Only show-size plants should be moved from a 4- to a 5-inch container. Overpotting is a common cause of failure with African violets.

A recommended soil mixture consists of 2 parts packaged potting soil and 1 part perlite.

Pruning: African violets have a natural shape and symmetry that should not be tampered with. Leaves that yellow or turn brown can be cut off close to the stem with a pair of manicure scissors. Spent flower stalks can be removed the same way. If a flower stalk has spent blossoms in addition to unopened buds, just pick off the faded flowers with your fingernails. It is best to groom plants just before they need watering. At this point, the leaf stalks are more flaccid than usual and less likely to snap when handled, a frustrating occurrence.

Many African violet hybrids sucker freely. That is, they produce little offsets from around the base of the mother plant. As these suckers grow, they destroy the plant's natural symmetry. Check regularly for the development of suckers and cut them off with small scissors as close to the main stem as possible or gently pull them out of the soil.

SPECIAL HINTS

When African violet leaves rest on the rim of a clay pot, they soon wither and die. Either the pot rim cuts the leaf stalk, or the fertilizer salts that accumulate in the clay cause damage. Growers who prefer clay to plastic containers often dip the pot rim into hot paraffin to prevent the problem. Plastic pots do not cause this problem.

There are available in some shops and through many mail-order companies gizmos called African violet rings. The ring fits around the rim of the flowerpot, and the outer circle of foliage rests on the ring, which holds the leaves up and out, helping to show them off and to maintain a flattened rosette. (They will also prevent the leaves from being damaged by the rim of a clay pot.)

Dust often becomes trapped between the leaf hairs of African violets. A gentle washing with plain tap water using a sink sprayer or hand atomizer helps keep the foliage clean and functioning efficiently. After washing, tilt and shake the plant so that any excess water spills off. Plants should not be placed in bright natural light until the leaves dry, or spotting may occur.

CHRISTMAS CACTUS

The Christmas cactus is one of nature's most beguiling achievements. Satiny-petaled flowers dangling from the tips of oddly segmented stems make this plant one of the season's best gifts.

DESCRIPTION

The Christmas cactus is a multistemmed plant; each of the dark green stems is segmented at 1- to 2-inch intervals. Tiered flowers are borne on the ends of the stems, giving the plant a graceful, arching appearance. Christmas cactuses are available in a wide range of colors including lilac, deep rose, salmon, red-orange, and white. Often the blossoms are bicolored, normally a combination of white and a pastel.

CHRISTMAS CACTUS

PLANT CARE DURING THE HOLIDAY SEASON

Light: Plants purchased in bud or bloom should be exposed to bright indirect sunlight during the flowering period; too much sun will cause flowers to fade before their time. "Bright indirect light" is a vague and often misunderstood term. It can be interpreted to mean placement directly in front of an unobstructed northern window; in front of a window facing east, west, or south, as long as translucent curtains are kept closed or Venetian blinds are partially drawn during the sunniest hours of the day; or at a window facing east, west, or south, where strong light is obstructed by a neighboring building or trees outside the window.

Temperature: During the blooming period night temperatures of 60° to 65° F. and day temperatures around 70° F. are ideal.

Moisture: Almost all problems with Christmas cactus can be traced to improper watering. Water thoroughly when the top half of soil in the pot feels very dry to the touch. Discard the excess water that accumulates in the drip plate beneath the container about 15 minutes after watering.

Placement in the Home: When the Christmas cactus is in bud, especially at the stage when buds are showing color but are still fairly small, leave the plant in bright indirect light. Moving it at this time to show it off is a common cause of bud drop. Once the flowers have opened, you can move it for a few days, to where you think it looks best, then bring it back into bright indirect light.

Plant Care Following the Holiday Season

Light, Temperature, and Moisture: Showcase specimens, the Christmas cactuses that really thrive, are exposed to higher light intensities than bright indirect for most of the year. Plants should be placed in front of the sunniest window in the house at all times except during the summer and when they are flowering. In summer, when the sun's rays are really strong, give them bright indirect light. Too much light during the dead of summer causes stems to become flaccid, faded, and scorched.

From Christmas until autumn continue to provide 60° to 70° F. night temperatures and day temperatures of 70° F. Starting in the autumn, encourage blooms for Christmas time by providing night temperatures around 55° F. Water when the top half of soil in the container feels dry to the touch.

Future Holiday Seasons

Christmas cactus will flower if night temperatures are low. Providing night temperatures of 50° to 55° F. from early November until the plants set bud is all it takes. The average indoor temperatures during the day are just fine.

Plants kept on the windowsill may automatically be exposed to low night temperatures. The portion of the plant closest to the window sets buds first, since it is exposed to lower temperatures than the inside half. At that point, turn the plant around, and buds will eventually set all over. This results in a succession of opening buds and an extended blooming period.

If you don't have a cool window, all is not lost. You can still force plants into bloom if night temperatures are in the 55° to 70° F. range, by subjecting them to 14 hours of total uninterrupted darkness every day, from the middle of October until buds set. Instructions for providing a dark period are included in the discussion on poinsettias (pp. 24-25).

Potting and Soil: Christmas cactuses seem to grow best in clay pots. This probably stems from the fact that soil dries faster in clay pots than in plastic ones. Christmas cactus may be moved from a plastic to a clay container, a practice not recommended for many other plants.

When necessary, repot into a container that is 1 to 1½ inches larger in diameter than the old pot. The mix should be 2 parts packaged potting soil and 1 part vermiculite or a coarse grade of builder's sand well speckled with gravel.

Fertilizing: The Christmas cactus grows most actively from early spring through the summer. This is the time to fertilize. Apply any of the products recommended for use on flowering houseplants, following the directions on the package label to the letter. There is no need to fertilize during the flowering period.

Pruning: After it has flowered, prune the Christmas cactus by cutting off a few of the "links" or sections from each stem tip. You can pinch them off with a fingernail or a pair of scissors to ensure a clean cut. Pruning encourages branching and the production of more stem tips, each having the potential to bear a flower.

SELECTION

Pick a Christmas cactus bearing large, ready-to-open buds. They are more likely to stay on the plant. Tiny buds seem to drop off between store and home in rebellion to the change of environment.

Choose a plant with firm stems that are a rich, green color, not puckered, curled, yellow, or brown — all indications of a moisture problem, either too much or not enough.

CYCLAMEN

Cyclamen has everything: large, exquisite flowers that contrast dramatically with truly handsome patterned leaves, plus a blooming period of several months. But beauty has its price. Cyclamen is often the most expensive plant available during the Christmas season

DESCRIPTION

People compare cyclamen flowers to butterflies, birds in flight, falling stars, and other natural wonders. They are available in white and shades of pink, red, and lavender. Cyclamen blossoms rise on long stalks above heart-shaped leaves that are exquisitely decorated with silvery or light green markings. If plants are properly tended, the flowers open in succession from December through April.

CYCLAMEN

Cyclamens come in two sizes and, consequently, two price ranges. The large and most showy varieties reach a height and width of about 12 inches. The "mini" forms attain half that size and are ideal when space and funds are limited.

Selection

Selecting a cyclamen is a simple matter. Just pick the plant with the greatest number of flower buds. The buds are hidden down in the center of the plant, so you will have to move a few leaves around to check it out. What you should find are buds in various stages of development — some almost tall enough to poke through the foliage, others just hovering above the corm (root). Do not worry about the number of fully opened flowers; those will come later. As always, be on the lookout for anything crawling and keep a special eye out for the presence of cyclamen mites.

Plant Care During the Holiday Season

Cool temperatures are the key to prolonging a cyclamen's bloom. The higher the temperature, the shorter the time a cyclamen will stay in top shape.

Light: Provide the cyclamen with as much light as possible by placing it in front of the sunniest window in your home. Many people worry unnecessarily about foliage burn on plants kept too close to a window. There really is no such thing as too much light between late autumn and early spring.

Temperature: Cyclamen prefers night temperatures in the 40° to 50° F. range and day temperatures less than 68° F. You will probably have to place the plant in the coldest room you have — perhaps an inside porch or chilly entranceway will work well. If your home is too warm, the cyclamen will survive for a period of time and should certainly last through the holiday season; however, the blooming period may be cut very short, and the foliage will yellow earlier than normal.

Moisture: Water when the top layer of soil in the container feels dry to the touch. Pour water just inside the rim of the pot, not into the center of the foliage. Always water thoroughly, until

Availability

Cyclamen lovers seek this plant during the Christmas season, when it's most easily found. Occasionally, you see cyclamen offered before December, but avoid buying one of the early birds. It is likely to have been overforced by an anxious grower in a rush to get it to market, and plants grown too quickly may not survive.

water runs through the drainage holes in the bottom of the container. Then wait about 15 minutes and discard the excess water that has accumulated in the drip plate beneath the pot.

Fertilizer: Fertilize plants every 2 weeks with a water-soluble chemical fertilizer recommended for use on indoor plants. A product with an analysis of 15-30-15 is ideal.

Placement in the Home: It is unlikely that the coolest room in your home is where you want to show off the cyclamen at its peak of color. It is perfectly acceptable to move the plant into the living room while entertaining or use it as a centerpiece on the dining room table. Just remember to return it to the cool growing area before going to bed at night, and make sure it receives as much light as possible at other times.

Plant Care Following the Holiday Season

It is not an easy task to carry over a cyclamen, but at appropriate temperatures it can be done.

Light, Temperature, Moisture, and Fertilizer: Continue to provide as much light as possible. Keep night temperatures between the 40s and low 50s; day temperatures should be less than 68° F. In summer it may not be possible to keep the growing area this cool—just place the plant in a spot that's well ventilated. Fertilize every 2 weeks as described above.

Throughout the blooming period, continue to water when the top layer of soil begins to feel dry. In March or April the plant will stop blooming, and the leaves will begin to yellow. The cyclamen will enter a dormant state, and the corm will undergo a ripening process, an essential part of its growth cycle. At this point, you should only water enough to

Future Holiday Seasons

During the summer, check regularly to see if the plants need watering, and continue to water only enough to keep the soil from completely drying out and the corm from shriveling. There is no need to fertilize until new growth begins.

When you see new leaves emerging from the corm, which will probably occur at the end of the summer, move the plant back to the spot where you had it originally and provide the same care as described with regard to light, temperature, moisture, and fertilizing. There is no need to provide short days as with poinsettias and kalanchoes in order to get the plants to bloom.

keep the soil from completely drying out and the corm from shriveling. As a result of this dry treatment, all the foliage will turn completely brown and will eventually fall from the corm, a process which may take up to 2 months. Do not pull the leaves off prematurely, because a piece of the corm may also be pulled off, leaving it vulnerable to infection and disease.

By the time the cyclamen is totally without foliage, it will be about May or June. At this time, you can move the plant to a less obtrusive spot until new growth begins, which should be by the end of summer. Many people place the potted cyclamen corm outdoors for the summer, claiming that the new growth is sturdier and that the plants fare better than those left inside.

Potting and Soil: After all the leaves have fallen and before you place the plant outside, repot the corm into a container that is 1 inch larger in diameter than the old pot. The top half of the corm should be placed above the soil line; the bottom half should be below ground. This will help ensure adequate drainage and avoid corm rot caused by moisture accumulation.

A soil mixture of 2 parts packaged potting soil, 1 part peat moss, and 1 part perlite is ideal. It is rich enough to support a healthy plant, and it drains well.

Pruning: Cyclamens are not generally pruned or shaped. The only growth that should be removed are leaves that have yellowed or turned brown. Leaves should not be pulled off. Instead, cut them off at the bottom, a bit above the corm, or wait for them to drop naturally.

KALANCHOE

KALANCHOE

The kalanchoe is the most mispronounced houseplant in the land. The proper pronunciation of this increasingly popular flowering beauty is ka-lan-KO-e. It rolls off the tongue in a pleasant, melodic way.

The kalanchoe is a member of the Crassula family, a widely grown group of succulents represented in most indoor gardens by the ever-popular jade plant and in most outdoor displays by the echeverias, commonly known as hen-and-chickens.

DESCRIPTION

Kalanchoes bear a canopy of garnet red, orange, yellow, or salmon flowers above a dome of thick, waxy green leaves. The richly colored flowers give the plant an umbrellalike appearance from afar. Close up, you can see the hundreds of starlike blossoms comprising the canopy. There are spectacular tall-growing varieties which reach about 1 foot in height, as well as mini forms about half that size.

Like other succulents, kalanchoes store water in their leaves and stems, the way cacti do, though not in the same quantity. For this reason, kalanchoes are reasonably drought-resistant and thus good choices for forgetful waterers.

AVAILABILITY

The kalanchoe blooms naturally when nights are long and days are short, making winter its general time of availability. Commercial growers, however, cleverly trick the plants into bloom during any season by hanging black cloth over the plants for 14 hours each day. Though seen in shops most often during the Christmas season, kalanchoes may also be found in full bloom for Valentine's Day and during the autumn holidays.

PLANT CARE DURING THE HOLIDAY SEASON

Light: The kalanchoe, like other succulents, requires abundant sunshine to retain its compact growth habit. You should provide a minimum of 4 hours of direct light each day by placing the plant in front of a sunny window.

Temperature: Like most winter bloomers, kalanchoes grow best where it is cool. Night temperatures of 50° to 60° F. and day temperatures of 65° to 70° F. will help ensure the longest possible blooming period and promote a stocky growth habit.

Moisture: Water the kalanchoe when the top half of the soil in the container feels dry to the touch. The frequency with which this occurs depends on several factors, so you must rely on your sense of touch, not the calendar, to tell you when it is time to break out the watering can. As with other pot plants, always water thoroughly until water runs through the drainage holes in the bottom of the container and empty the saucer after 15 minutes. Overwatering causes stem rot at the soil line — the leading cause of death among houseplant succulents. If your kalanchoe turns yellow, it was most likely overwatered. At that point the plant is probably irretrievable.

SELECTION

Choose a plant with most of the flowers still unopened, not one in full bloom.

Select a specimen that is compact, not one with long spaces between the leaves. A leggy plant may have been grown under higher-than-recommended temperatures or lower-than-optimum light levels.

Pick a kalanchoe with plump, fleshy leaves. Wrinkled or puckered foliage indicates improper watering, and you may never get the plant to look quite right.

Fertilizer: If plants are purchased in bloom, there is no need to fertilize until the flowering period is over and new growth has begun. Otherwise, fertilize with a product recommended for houseplants as soon as you see new leaves developing.

Placement in the Home: Everyone wants to show off a plant that is in full flower, and nothing adorns the coffee table or mantle like a kalanchoe blooming its head off in December or January. In the evening or anytime after you have provided its 4 hours a day of direct sunlight, feel free to move the plant wherever you like — just remember to return it to the window the next morning.

Plant Care Following the Holiday Season

Light, Temperature, Moisture, and Fertilizer: Continue to provide a minimum of 4 hours of direct sunlight each day. Cool temperatures should still be maintained in order to keep plants sturdy and compact. Continue to water thoroughly when the top half of soil in the pot feels dry.

When you see new growth, it is time to begin fertilizing. Any of the fertilizers labeled for use on flowering houseplants is suitable, as long as the directions are carefully followed with regard to frequency and amount of application.

Potting and Soil: Kalanchoes are usually repotted after flowering. Select a container 1 to 1½ inches larger in diameter than the old one. A soil mix composed of equal parts packaged potting soil and sand works well. Do not use fine sand or beach sand, but a coarse grade of builder's sand — the type with little bits of gravel scattered throughout.

Pruning: After plants have flowered, cut back each stem below the flower stalk and just above a node, the point where a leaf joins the stem. During the active growing period, usually between early spring and late summer, pinch back each growing tip by cutting off a pair or two of leaves. This encourages branching and produces a full specimen with a multitude of growing tips, each capable of bearing a tuft of blossoms. Use sharp shears to assure a clean, unjagged cut.

Future Holiday Seasons

Though kalanchoes are short-day plants, blooming in their native lands when nights are long, they usually flower under average indoor conditions during spring. For Christmas flowering they must be subjected to 14 hours of total uninterrupted darkness daily, with as much light as possible in between, from September 1 to early October. Providing a dark period as described in the poinsettia section (pp. 24-25) is imperative. But keep in mind that the number of weeks that the dark period is necessary is shorter for kalanchoes than for poinsettias.

If you are satisfied with a spring-blooming kalanchoe, just tend the plant as described above and let nature take its course.

Poinsettia

The poinsettia has become the nation's most popular gift plant. Its bright red bracts and green leaves signify the Christmas season; it is given as a decorative Yuletide houseplant and used as a source of cut flowers for holiday arrangements. In warm regions of the country, including Florida and Hawaii, the poinsettia is a common flowering shrub.

Description

What most people think of as the flower petals of a poinsettia are really colored leaves called *bracts*. The true flowers are the insignificant greenish "buttons" found in the center of the bracts.

Because poinsettias are so popular, breeders continue to work on improving them. In recent years they have developed varieties with shocking pink, mauve, orange, and even bicolored bracts, in addition to the more common red and white.

POINSETTIA

It is widely believed that poinsettias are poisonous. The fact is, where plant parts have been eaten, some rare instances of local irritation (stomach pains with vomiting and diarrhea) have been documented. Since small children are often attracted to the poinsettia's bright colors, it is a good idea to keep the plant out of harm's way. In addition, poinsettias contain a milky white sap in both stems and leaves. When the plant is cut, the sap oozes freely and may cause a poison-ivy-like reaction or severe eye irritation on contact. You should exercise care when pruning or potting.

Availability

Poinsettias appear in the marketplace as early as Thanksgiving. Retail outlets generally feature and sell the plants until Christmas, but you will be hard pressed to find a poinsettia for sale at any other time of year, particularly a good-looking one. It is best to buy early before the pickings become slim.

Poinsettias are fussy. Without proper care, plants may not last through the season in top form.

Light: Poinsettias need 3 to 4 hours of direct sunlight daily, which can be achieved by placing the plant in front of a sunny window.

Temperature: Poinsettias stay freshest in a cool room. If it is too hot, lower leaves may suddenly drop, and plants will look faded and lackluster. Night temperatures of 55° to 65° F. and day temperatures of 65° to 70° F. are ideal.

Moisture: Water your poinsettia when the top layer of soil in the container feels clearly dry to the touch. Always water thoroughly, until the water runs through the drainage holes in the bottom of the pot. Wait about 15 minutes and then discard any excess water that has accumulated in the drip plate beneath the container.

Since the poinsettia is native to a moist, subtropical climate, humidity should be increased if plants are kept where temperatures exceed those recommended. If necessary, place the plant on a large saucer or tray filled with constantly moistened pebbles or pea gravel. Do not allow the water level in the tray to go above the top layer of pebbles, since plants sitting in water often suffer root damage.

Fertilizer: Commercial growers keep poinsettias on a regular fertilizer schedule for months before sending them to the marketplace. There is no need for you to add more nutrients until early spring.

Placement in the Home: Never place poinsettias in a draft — whether from a window, doorway, or heating unit. When placing plants in front of a window, take care to prevent the leaves or bracts from touching cold window-panes.

SELECTION

In larger nurseries, or even supermarkets, you may have hundreds of poinsettias to choose from. To choose the best poinsettia out of a crowd, keep the following points in mind:

■ Choose a plant with leaves down to the bottom of the stems. This indicates the plant has been well cared for and has an active and healthy root system.

■ Pick a poinsettia with flower bracts and leaves that are fresh looking, not wrinkled, withered, curled, or yellow — all signs of a lack of water or a possible nutrient deficiency.

■ Look for a plant with a few upper bracts that still show a trace of green. That means that the plant's peak of perfection is yet to come.

■ Avoid buying a plant that has exuded sap from leaves or stems.

Most people do not want to bother with the poinsettia after Christmas — and for good reason. Its care is time-consuming, and forcing it to bloom for the following Christmas can be tricky. If you think your time would be better spent on other gardening tasks, do not feel guilty. Keep and care for your plant until the bracts have dropped and then, with a free conscience, throw it out or give it to a friend who might be more inclined to deal with it.

On the other hand, if you want to try to carry your poinsettia over for next Christmas, the following paragraphs will help you succeed. A properly tended plant becomes larger and more beautiful each year, so successfully bringing one into bloom for a second time has its rewards. Proper care should ensure the life and health of your plant for many years to come.

Light, Temperature, Moisture, and Fertilizer: After the bracts have dropped off, continue to provide the poinsettia with at least 4 hours of direct sunlight each day by keeping it directly in front of a bright window. Cool temperatures, 55° to 65° F. at night and 65° to 70° F. during the day, should be maintained. Naturally, in the summer your home will be a bit warmer — that is perfectly acceptable. Continue to water the plant thoroughly when the top layer of soil feels dry to the touch. Provide a pebble tray if temperatures are much higher than suggested. The tray is a far more effective way to raise humidity in a dry room than misting plants with an atomizer. Just do not let the water level in the tray touch the bottom of pots.

When the plant begins to make new growth, likely in early spring, begin applying a water-soluble chemical fertilizer as directed on the package label. A product with a composition of 15-30-15 is ideal.

Potting and Soil: Your poinsettia is ready for a larger container if you see roots growing through the drainage holes in the bottom of the pot, when the soil dries unusually fast between waterings, or when water runs through the soil more quickly than in the past.

Select a new container which is 1 to 1½ inches larger in diameter than the old one. A plant that jumps from a 4-inch pot to a 7-inch pot often suffers because the overabundance of soil around the roots tends to stay wet too long and root rot may result. Most poinsettias are sold in plastic pots and should be repotted into plastic. If the initial container is clay, stick with clay so that the finicky poinsettia will not have to make any more adjustments than necessary.

A suitable growing medium consists of equal parts packaged potting soil and perlite.

Pruning: Plants should be pruned after the flower bracts have begun to drop. Prune stems to a height of 6 to 8 inches without worrying whether any leaves remain. In a few weeks new growth will commence. This may seem drastic, but it is guaranteed to result in a far superior specimen in the long run. Without pruning, your plant is apt to become an overgrown, bare-legged, gawky specimen, bearing little resemblance to the one you purchased or received as a gift. All pruning cuts should be made cleanly just above a node, the point where a leaf is attached to the stem. After pruning, return the plant to its sunny windowsill and continue to water and fertilize as recommended.

Future Christmases

After all danger of frost has passed, the poinsettia should be placed outside in a spot that gets the morning sun but is sheltered from the hot afternoon rays. (Check with your local Cooperative Extension Service for the latest recorded frost date in your area.) Bury the pot in the ground up to its rim so the roots will stay cooler and the plant will not blow over in the wind or rain. If you live in an apartment and cannot move the plant outside, leave it on its sunny windowsill and continue to care for it as if it were outside. During summer, pinch back the growing tips every few weeks to produce a bushy multiflowered plant for the next Christmas season. Continue to fertilize as recommended on the label of the product used. Plants placed outdoors will require frequent watering — every day if the weather is warm and dry. Check daily to see if your plant needs watering by poking your finger into the soil.

If all goes well, by autumn you will have a large, well-branched specimen with several growing tips, each with the potential to bear colored bracts. Before the danger of the season's first frost, or by October 1, whichever comes first, bring your plant back inside. It is likely that it will need repotting at this time.

Once indoors, the poinsettia should be subjected to 14 hours of *total* uninterrupted darkness and given as much direct sunlight as possible in between. Finding a spot that is totally dark for 14 hours may present a problem. Obvious choices are a closet, spare room, or cellar. But if the closet is frequently opened at night in search of a hat or coat, if laundry is done in the cellar after nightfall, or if the spare-room door is left ajar, you should avoid such areas.

In the event that an appropriate spot does not exist in your home, the plant can be placed each evening inside a black plastic trash bag tied at the top. To prevent the plastic from touching the foliage, you can fashion hoops from wire coat hangers and anchor the ends in the soil. The hoops will hold the plastic above the leaves. Whether the poinsettia is kept in a spare room during the forcing period or placed inside a trash bag, you should continue to water thoroughly when the top layer of soil feels dry to the touch.

The fact that many dedicated gardeners fail to produce a blooming plant by Christmas can usually be attributed to one of three causes. First, the night temperature recommended for poinsettias is between 55° F. and 65° F. Closets, spare rooms, and the inside of a plastic bag tend to be too warm and stuffy. This causes leaf drop and may prevent flowering. So a cool room, whether or not the plant is inside a plastic bag, or a closet that backs onto an outside wall is essential. Second, total uninterrupted darkness is difficult to provide, and this crucial requirement often goes unfulfilled. Third, removing the plant from the dark each morning is an easily forgotten task. Abundant sunshine during the day is as important as total darkness at night.

Believe it or not, persistence has its reward. After you have moved the poinsettia from the dark to light and back again each day throughout the fall, color will begin to show in the bracts. At this point the shuttle is over, and the plant can be cared for in a cool, well-lit spot to adorn your home for another Christmas holiday and repay you for your efforts.

RIEGER BEGONIA

Rieger Begonia

The long-blooming Rieger begonias (pronounced Ryeger) are Christmas show stoppers. Their many varieties differ in color and flower form, but all have one common trait: a blooming period that can last for months.

Description

During the winter months, Rieger begonias produce a profusion of gorgeous blossoms in various shades of red, white, pink, yellow, rose, and orange. Some varieties have four-petaled flowers called "singles." These flowers look like the blossoms of a wax begonia but are larger and flashier. Other varieties produce multipetaled blossoms called "doubles," which are reminiscent of small camellia flowers or rose blossoms.

Plant Care During the Holiday Season

Riegers, like all begonias, have exacting requirements for care. The closer you can meet these requirements, the longer the blooming period will be — up to 4 months and sometimes longer. If your home is a little warm or dark, enjoy the plant for as long as the flowers last and forget about carrying it over, since this can be a tricky and frustrating business.

Light: During the flowering period, plants should be provided with bright indirect light, as described on page 13. Too much light at this time may cause the flowers to fade early. Too little may cause plants to stretch toward the light source and cease blooming earlier than they should.

Temperature: The Riegers not only prefer, but *require,* low night temperatures to stay in flower and retain their stocky growth habit. Night temperatures in the 50° F. range and day temperatures around 70° F. are excellent. A plant grown where it is too warm will soon become a gawky mess bearing little resemblance to the showpiece you acquired.

Moisture: Newly acquired plants should be watered when the top layer of soil feels dry to the touch. Always water thoroughly, until water runs through the drainage holes in the bottom of the container. Then wait about 15 minutes and discard any excess water that has accumulated in the drip plate beneath the pot. Be careful not to overwater, a common cause of begonia fatalities. Constantly wet soil creates a perfect breeding ground for fungi, to which the begonias are particularly susceptible. When watering Riegers, and for that matter all begonias, avoid splashing water on the foliage. Wet leaves are more prone to disease than dry ones.

Begonias grow best where humidity is between 40 and 60 percent. Since most homes are not this humid, especially during the winter months, place plants on a pebble tray (see page 6). The leaves of begonias grown in a dry room become crisp around the edges.

AVAILABILITY

Riegers flower all winter long and are sold throughout the blooming season. They are plentiful at both Christmas and Easter but scarce at other times of the year. The likeliest place to find Riegers is at florist shops or specialty stores.

Fertilizer: Blooming plants should be fertilized monthly with a water-soluble chemical fertilizer recommended for use on houseplants. A product with an analysis of 15-30-15 is ideal. Be sure to follow the package directions carefully.

CHAPTER 2
WINTER
PLANTS

PLANT CARE FOLLOWING THE HOLIDAY SEASON

Light, Temperature, Moisture, and Fertilizer: Continue to provide bright indirect light. Night temperatures in the 50° F. range and day temperatures around 70° F. should be maintained. Keep fertilizing every month. Water as before, when the top layer of soil in the container feels dry to the touch.

When all flowers have faded and there are no buds left on the plant, which for well-tended specimens may be up to 6 months after purchase, it is time for your Rieger to take a rest. Allow the soil to dry completely for 10 days. Then water only when the top *half* of the soil in the pot feels completely dry to the touch.

SELECTION

The toughest thing about selection, once you have found a source of Riegers, is choosing among them. When it comes to color and flower type, one hybrid is more glorious and alluring than the next. But do not choose on the basis of color or the number of flower petals alone. You also want a healthy plant. Here are a few tips:

- Begonias are prone to several foliage fungus diseases which cause yellow or brown spots and blotches on the leaves. Avoid buying a plant that shows any signs of trouble.

- Choose a stocky, well-branched specimen, not one that is leggy or spindly, which indicates that the plant was grown where temperatures were too high or light intensity too low.

- Though the flashiest plant in the shop will have all the flowers fully opened, the best buy is the one with plenty of buds in all stages of development. You want the plant at its peak of color in your home, not in the store.

Potting and Soil: An ideal growing medium consists of equal parts packaged potting soil, perlite, and vermiculite. When repotting Riegers, always set the old root ball ½ inch or so higher than the new soil line to assure good drainage and avoid root and stem

27

rot. It is time to repot Riegers after you have pruned the plants as described in the following paragraph. Repot into a container that is only 1 to 1½ inches larger in diameter than the old pot.

Pruning: After the 10-day dry period, prune the stems to 3 inches in height. The next crop of flowers will form on this new growth. Use a sharp knife or shears to assure a clean, unjagged cut. After pruning, remove any dead or diseased leaves from the soil surface and from the bottom of the plant.

A few times during the growing period that follows the rest, pinch off the stem tips, making all cuts just above a node, the place where a leaf joins the stem. This will encourage branching and promote bushy growth.

FUTURE HOLIDAY SEASONS

Continue to water plants only when the top half of soil in the container feels dry to the touch, until new growth appears. Then begin watering when just the top *layer* of soil feels dry.

Once plants have begun growing again, place them in front of a sunny window where they will receive 4 hours of direct sunlight each day. It is essential at this time that night temperatures be in the mid-50s and day temperatures be not higher than 70° F. Plants grown where it is too warm will be leggy, not stocky or bushy. Begin fertilizing every 2 weeks with the same water-soluble chemical fertilizer you were using before.

Plants should flower again in several months, though exactly how long this will take depends on growing conditions in your home. If you succeed, you'll really have something to be proud of.

Chapter 3

Spring Plants

Azalea

In parts of America where conditions encourage the successful cultivation of azaleas outdoors, everyone knows and loves them. There are, however, parts of the United States where azaleas do not grow well for one reason or another; either summers are too hot, winters are too cold, or soil conditions are inappropriate. For those living in azalea-growing territory, azaleas mean spring, so they are the perfect plant to commemorate the season.

Description

Though most azaleas are deciduous and can reach heights of up to 15 feet, the azaleas grown for houseplants are evergreen shrubs, generally up to 2 feet high. They have small, oval-oblong leaves and funnel-shaped flowers produced in clusters at the stem tips. There is a wide color range, including white and shades of pink, salmon, crimson, magenta, and orange, as well as several bicolored forms. Some have single, 5-petaled flowers; others bear double, multipetaled blossoms. Most azaleas bloom naturally in early spring but can be forced for earlier flowering or held back to bloom at a later date.

AZALEA

Azaleas are classified into various groups. The type most often grown in greenhouses as a houseplant or gift plant is nicknamed Indian azalea and also large-flowered azalea, since its blossoms are up to 3 inches across. They are not hardy outdoors except in the very warmest parts of the country.

Cultural Requirements

The most common mistake made with newly acquired azaleas is underwatering. Most plants found in shops are fairly pot-bound, since they flower most heavily in undersized containers. As a result, the soil tends to dry out rapidly between waterings. If not kept properly moistened, plants will droop miserably and shed leaves at a horrifying rate. Other azalea care is relatively straightforward.

Light: Since azaleas require 4 hours of very bright light each day, placing the plant close to a window is essential. A northern exposure that receives indirect light will do nicely. A southern or eastern exposure where the sun's strong afternoon rays are filtered through sheer curtains or partially closed shutters also works.

Temperature: Night temperatures of 45° to 55° F. and day temperatures of 68° F. or less are perfect to prolong flower freshness and keep your plant in top form.

SELECTION

When buying a plant, you want to select a healthy, vigorous specimen with a bushy growth habit, rich, green, unmarred foliage, and a generous supply of unopened flower buds. You should not have much trouble finding a worthy specimen, but you must be on the lookout for a number of problems to which azaleas are prone. These are major maladies to beware of:

- The wilt organisms that affect azaleas cause young leaves to yellow and droop. If the soil is moist and leaves have wilted, suspect a problem and continue your search.

- Flower spot or azalea petal blight produces pale, circular, pinhead-sized spots on the undersides of infected flower petals. Eventually the spots enlarge and grow together, creating white blotches on colored flowers and brown blotches on white blossoms. Ultimately the entire flower collapses.

- A number of fungi cause discolored, irregularly shaped leaf spots on azaleas. In severe cases leaves will drop. Leaf yellowing often occurs when plants are grown in overly alkaline soil, which ties up available iron and causes discoloration. Beware also of spider mites, aphids, whiteflies, mealybugs, and scale insects .

Moisture: Check daily to see if the top layer of soil in the container feels dry to the touch. If so, soak thoroughly by pouring water into the soil until it runs through the drainage holes in the bottom of the pot. Wait about 15 minutes and *again* water thoroughly. Discard any excess moisture that accumulates in the drip plate beneath the pot about 30 minutes after the double soaking.

Fertilizer: There is no need to fertilize an azalea while it is in bloom.

Placement in the Home: Since this plant requires low night temperatures, it will probably have to be set in a cool entranceway or enclosed porch during the evening. However, when entertaining, feel free to move it to where it can be seen. No harm will be done as long as it is returned within a day or so to an area where conditions are appropriate.

Plant Care After Flowers Fade

Azaleas can be carried over from year to year, becoming larger and more full of flowers with time. They do, however, require cool growing conditions, a problem for gardenless gardeners to provide. Perhaps apartment dwellers would be better off giving their azaleas to a home-owning friend once the flowers have faded.

Light, Temperature, Moisture, and Fertilizer: After the azalea has bloomed, provide 4 hours of direct sunlight daily. Maintain temperatures of 45° to 55° F. or lower by day. Water as described when the top layer of soil begins to feel dry.

Begin fertilizing with an acid-type fertilizer recommended for use on azaleas every 2 weeks from the time the flowers fade until late summer, when new flower buds form. Withhold fertilizer after that point. If the leaves on your azalea turn yellow between the veins, apply a chelated iron product (available at garden centers) according to package directions.

AVAILABILITY

Since it is possible for commercial growers to have azaleas in flower year-round, a search of major garden centers and florist shops should uncover a source at any season. Plants are most plentiful, however, around Easter and Mother's Day, and also around Christmas and Valentine's Day, when red-flowered varieties dominate.

Potting and Soil: After plants bloom, pinch off the faded blossoms and repot into a new container that is 1 inch larger in diameter than the old pot. Be sure not to overpot; azaleas flower best in tight containers. A mixture of 2 parts peat moss, 1 part packaged potting soil, and 1 part builder's sand or perlite is suitable.

Placing the Azalea Temporarily Outdoors: In cooler parts of the country, where evergreen azaleas will not survive winter temperatures, they should be placed temporarily outdoors during warm weather. After the danger of frost has passed, plunge the pot up to its rim in a well-drained spot that receives morning sunlight and dappled shade during the afternoon. Remember to fertilize every 2 weeks until buds form at the end of summer. Water plants during dry spells. Shrubs in containers plunged into the earth dry more quickly than those in open soil, since the roots have no place to go in search of moisture. It is therefore necessary to check the soil frequently during hot, dry periods. **Bringing Plants Back Inside in Autumn:** Unless you live in Zone 8, 9, or 10, the Indian azaleas must be overwintered indoors. Before the danger of autumn frost, bring azaleas that would not survive the winter in your area back inside. Place them in a cool, sunny spot where temperatures are in the 45° to 55° F. range. Warmer temperatures are one of the major reasons people get a skimpy supply of flowers. Once the flower buds are well formed and show color, plants can be moved into a warmer room during the day. Once in bloom, provide azaleas with the same care as described above.

Pruning: To ensure bushy, well-branching growth, azaleas should be shaped and pruned annually, immediately after they finish blooming. If this job is delayed, you may unwittingly cut off next year's flower buds. The pinching off of spent blossoms and the annual pruning should be performed concurrently.

An Important Tip

Indoors, developing azalea buds should be misted with warm water to keep the calyx soft, so that the buds can emerge easily and without deformity. (The calyx consists of the *sepals* or leaflike structures that initially enclose the flower buds and eventually lie under them.)

There is another pruning chore often recommended for growing professional-quality azaleas. It is the removal of the tiny green shoots that develop around and often cover new flower buds. Some professionals believe that this growth should be removed as soon as it appears because it diverts nutrients from the buds and may cause them to dry before opening, and because it hides the flowers. A second flush of growth should appear after the plants flower, and this growth should be left alone since it will carry the following year's blossoms.

CALCEOLARIA AND CINERARIA

These two dramatic and novel plants are botanically unrelated, yet the similarity of their cultural requirements warrant joint treatment in this book.

These two plants have some important characteristics in common. Both require low temperatures to stay fresh as long as possible; both are treated as annuals and discarded after their flowers fade; and the sight of either of them in full bloom is a treat you will not soon forget.

The calceolaria bears large, slightly hairy, soft leaves, up to 6 inches long, on plants usually less than 1 foot high. The

Full-page photo: *Hydrangea macrophylla.* MAGGIE OSTER. **Inset: White florist's cyclamen.** DAVID M. STONE: PHOTO/NATS.

Full page photo: Assorted cyclamens *(Cyclamen persicum)*. JOHN A. LYNCH: PHOTO/NATS. **Inset, above: Christmas cactus.** JOHN A. LYNCH: PHOTO/ NATS. **Inset, opposite page: Cattleya orchid, 'Lavender Valentine'.** MAGGIE OSTER.

Full-page photo: **Amaryllis and other bulbs forced indoors.** JERRY HOWARD/POSITIVE IMAGES. **Inset, above: White cattleya orchid.** PRISCILLA CONNELL: PHOTO/NATS. **Inset, opposite page: Amaryllis.** JERRY HOWARD/POSITIVE IMAGES.

Full-page photo: Primrose *(Primula)*. JERRY HOWARD/POSITIVE IMAGES. **Inset, top: Rose pincushion cactus *(Mammillaria Zeilmanniana cristata)*.** DAVID M. STONE: PHOTO/ NATS. **Inset, above: Cape primrose *(Streptocarpus* hybrid).** ANN REILLY: PHOTO/ NATS.

Full-page photo: Crown-of-thorns (*Euphorbia milii*). MAGGIE OSTER. **Inset: Purple gloxinia.** SYDNEY KARP: PHOTO/NATS.

unusual pouchlike flowers, about 2 inches across, are produced in a stunning bouquet above the foliage. Calceolaria blossoms are reminiscent of a lady's handbag (hence their most popular nickname, pocketbook plant) and they are as soft as Italian suede. Flower colors include red, pink, maroon, bronze, and yellow — the latter being the most frequently seen. They are often speckled with brown, purple, or red.

Cinerarias also bear hairy leaves, 3 to 4 inches long, that are green on top and gray-purple below, on plants about 1 foot high. They produce a glorious massed head of rich-colored, daisylike flowers above the foliage. The flowers, 1 to 4 inches across, may be white or the richest shades of pink, red, blue, or violet, often contrasted by white centers.

CALCEOLARIA

Availability

Calceolarias are most available around the Easter holidays, though plants may be found as late as Mother's Day. Cinerarias are most often found in the shops from January through April.

CINERARIA

Cultural Requirements

The care of calceolarias and cinerarias is remarkably similar, as are the cultural mistakes made with them. The most common error is keeping these cool growers in too warm a spot.

Light: Both plants should be placed in bright indirect light while in flower (see page 13). Too much light will cause the leaves to wilt and turn brown and the flowers to fade.

Temperature: Night temperatures of 40° to 45° F. and day temperatures of 55° to 60° F. are perfect. Set these plants in a very cool spot, such as an entranceway, unheated porch, or cool bay window.

Moisture: Water both plants thoroughly when the top layer of soil feels dry to the touch. Since calceolarias and cinerarias tend to dry out very quickly between waterings, check them daily to see if irrigation is required. Avoid splashing water on the foliage because the leaves tend to spot. To avoid stem rot, never pour

33

water into the center of either plant. Instead, place the spout of your watering can just inside the rim of the pot.

Fertilizer: These plants do not require fertilizer while in bloom.

Placement in the Home: Avoid placing these plants in drafty areas. Appropriately low temperatures are mandatory, however; placement of these plants in a cool room is essential to their endurance.

SELECTION

When buying either of these plants, select a specimen with plenty of flowers still to open, so that the peak of perfection will be reached at home, not in the shop. Most of the calceolarias and cinerarias available are in pretty good shape, but there are a few problems to keep an eye out for:

■ Calceolarias are prone to a yellowing of the leaf tips which results from inadequate soil drainage, overwatering, or overfertilizing.

■ Stem rot — resulting from plants being potted too deep, poor drainage, or overwatering — can also be a problem. Before you buy, check the base of the plant for soft spots.

■ Aphids, spider mites, and especially whiteflies are crazy about both plants; watch out for these pests.

■ Beware of drooping plants potted in well-moistened soil, a symptom of wilt disease, to which cinerarias are subject.

PLANT CARE AFTER FLOWERS FADE

Now for the darker side of the calceolaria/cineraria story. Both of these plants are, from a practical point of view, annuals. They are grown from seed for winter or spring bloom and then discarded. To try and carry them over is a colossal waste of time and energy. There is no comparison in quality between a seed-grown plant and one dragged over from one Easter to the next. After the flowers die, out they must go.

EASTER LILY

Easter lilies are to Easter what poinsettias are to Christmas — living symbols of the holiday. As the red bracts and green foliage of a poinsettia represent the Christmas color scheme, the snow-white flowers of an Easter lily commemorate the purity of Easter and herald the coming of spring. And, like their Yuletide counterparts, they are raised by the millions every year by commercial growers who carefully coax them into bloom for Easter gift-giving.

Description

The sweetly scented, funnel-shaped white flowers of the Easter lily are 6 to 8 inches long and 4 to 5 inches wide. The flowers are produced atop leafy stems, 1 to 3 feet high.

Easter lilies are among the hundreds of lily species, flowering plants prized for their unsurpassed beauty, stately habit, and gorgeously colored, delicate blossoms. All lilies grow from a bulb composed of fleshy scales, not from a solid structure like the tulip bulb. Most lilies flower in summer (including the Easter lily, which is artificially forced for spring bloom). All lilies are perennial. They produce foliage in spring, flower in summer, and die back to the ground during winter, a cycle repeated annually.

EASTER LILY

Cultural Requirements

There is nothing complicated about caring for a newly acquired Easter lily. Nevertheless, it is important to remember that, as with other bulbous plants, too much moisture can cause the speedy and untimely demise of this beauty.

Light: An Easter lily in bloom should be provided with bright indirect light such as that found in front of a northern window. A sunnier exposure, where the bright afternoon sun is filtered through sheer curtains, partially closed Venetian blinds, or shrubs growing outside the window, is also suitable.

Temperature: Night temperatures of 45° to 60° F. and day temperatures of 68° F. or lower are ideal for prolonging flower freshness.

Moisture: Water thoroughly only when the top layer of soil feels very dry to the touch, not before. Too much water may cause the bulb to rot.

Fertilizer: There is no need to fertilize an Easter lily while it is in bloom.

Placement in the Home: Since the Easter lily does best with low night temperatures, you may need to place it on an unheated porch or in a cool entranceway during the night. It can be moved to the living area during the day — just remember to provide appropriate light levels.

Plant Care After Flowers Fade

Caring for an Easter lily after it has flowered entails the same basic principles as maintaining other bulb plants. The flowers should be pinched off after they fade, but the flower stalk and foliage are left intact to produce the nutrients for next

SELECTION

Most Easter lilies found in the marketplace are of wonderfully high quality, but there are a few points you should keep in mind when making a selection in order to get the best buy:

■ To get the longest possible show from an Easter lily, select a plant with one or two lower flowers opened and the upper buds just beginning to show the white color of the blossoms.

■ Avoid plants that have lost lower leaves. This is usually caused by a lack of nitrogen, poor soil aeration, a lack of water, or overcrowding — a condition that results in light deficiency.

■ Aphids are the chief Easter-lily pest; check closely for infestation.

■ Avoid buying a plant with leaf-tip burn, a common problem caused by improper soil pH or a nutrient imbalance.

■ Select a plant with plenty of flower buds. A specimen that has produced less than the plant's potential number may have been grown from a puny bulb, a bulb stored too long before potting, or one allowed to dry out in storage. Check other plants in the shops for comparison, so you will know to avoid a sparsely budded specimen.

■ Do not buy a plant that shows signs of blight. This common disorder causes discolored circular or oval spots on leaves and flowers.

year's blossoms. If the green growth is removed, the bulb may come up "blind" the following year — without any flowers at all. **Light, Temperature, Moisture, and Fertilizer:** After the plant has bloomed, place it on a windowsill that receives a few hours of direct sunlight daily. Normal indoor temperatures are just fine.

Water exactly as you have been. After the flowers have been removed, fertilize every 2 weeks with a water-soluble chemical fertilizer recommended for use on flowering houseplants. Apply the product at one-half the strength suggested on the label.

Planting Outdoors: It is very difficult to carry over an Easter lily from one year to the next indoors, unless you have a greenhouse and some type of cool storage area. Assuming you do not, the best way to ensure the survival of your lily is to plant it outdoors in the garden. Set the Easter lily out among herbaceous perennials such as chrysanthemums, phlox, peonies, or, best of all, other lilies.

In the spring, after the danger of frost has passed, select a well-drained site in your garden. A spot that receives bright morning sun and partial shade during the afternoon is perfect. If the soil is heavy, add some organic matter, such as peat moss or leaf mold. It is also a good idea to add a slow-release organic fertilizer, such as steamed bonemeal, to the planting hole.

Remove the plant from its container, being extremely careful not to damage the roots. Set the Easter lily 2 to 3 inches deeper than it was placed in its container. Since the Easter lily is less hardy than most other bulbs, it will benefit from being placed deeper in the earth, where it is warmer. After planting, cut the lily back to half its size and water well. Afterwards, irrigate during dry spells.

In late autumn, mulch your plant heavily, especially where winters are severe. Wood chips, pine boughs, and dry leaves are great for keeping the ground warm and preventing the bulb from being heaved out of position from the alternate freezing and thawing of the soil during winter. At some point during the autumn the foliage will wither, as with any other perennial. In spring new leaves should appear, and the plant will bloom in summer.

GLOXINIA

Gloxinia

The gloxinia is a relative of the African violet. It has special cultural needs and requires more attention than its more famous cousin; while the African violet rewards its owner with several sets of blossoms each year in exchange for minimal care, the gloxinia bears a single flush of flowers after trying the patience of its owner. However, once you have seen a gloxinia in full bloom, any extra bother is sure to seem worthwhile.

DESCRIPTION

The beautiful flowers of gloxinias, 3 inches or more across, are either bell-shaped or slipper-shaped and are held on stiff stalks above the foliage. Colors include rich purple, deep red, white, lavender, and pink. Blossoms are often marked with a contrasting hue, in the form of either bands or speckles. There are single-flowered varieties as well as multipetaled double forms.

In addition to stupendous flowers, gloxinias produce velvety oval leaves, up to 8 inches across. Like African violets, a single plant may bear either a symmetrical rosette of foliage or several rosettes arranged in a helter-skelter pattern, depending on the variety and growing techniques.

Gloxinias grow from a tuber, a modified underground stem that looks like a bulb. Like most other tuberous plants, they require a rest between flowerings.

SELECTION

To get your money's worth out of a full-grown blooming plant, choose one with healthy leaves and plenty of unopened flower buds. Look for a compact growing habit. Plants that are stretched out and leggy were probably grown in poor light or overcrowded conditions. Check closely for spider mites on the undersides of leaves, and examine leaf axils for the presence of mealy bugs. Make sure there are no soft or rotten spots at the base of the plant where the stem meets the soil line. Select a plant that bears the full complement of leaves; gloxinia foliage is brittle, and leaves are easily broken in shipment.

CULTURAL REQUIREMENTS

Following are some simple instructions for the care of a gloxinia plant in bloom. Due to improper watering or too little light, most people do not get the full show from their plants. Special attention should be paid to these requirements.

Light: Gloxinias require at least 4 hours of very bright indirect natural light every day, or 12 to 14 hours of artificial fluorescent light. Insufficient light will cause leaves to stretch upward. Too much natural light in summer may cause scorching, though this is rarely a problem in other seasons. Plants grown on a windowsill should be given a quarter turn every week to prevent them from leaning toward the light and losing their natural symmetry.

The best gloxinias are grown under fluorescent light. Plants should be placed within 6 inches of a standard 4-foot, 2-tube fluorescent fixture equipped with one cool and one warm white

40-watt tube. Fluorescent light fixtures are available from hardware, garden-supply, or variety stores.

Temperature: Most growers recommend night temperatures of 65° to 70° F. and day temperatures of 75° F., but gloxinias can tolerate night winter temperatures down to 55° F. Naturally, plants must be slowly acclimated to such low temperatures.

Moisture: Irrigate when the top layer of soil in the container feels dry to the touch. Then water thoroughly until water runs through the drainage holes in the bottom of the pot. To prevent foliage discoloration and spotting, avoid splashing water on the leaves.

Since gloxinias grow best where relative humidity is in the 50 to 60 percent range, set pots on a pebble tray — a watertight tray filled with well-moistened pea gravel. The water will evaporate and humidify the air surrounding the plant.

AVAILABILITY

Though in nature they bloom in late summer, flowering gloxinia plants are most plentiful in the shops during late winter and early spring, making them popular for Easter and early spring gift-giving.

PLANT CARE AFTER FLOWERS FADE

Caring for a gloxinia after the flowers have faded entails allowing the plant to take a brief rest, forcing it to begin growing again, and, finally, providing the care that will ultimately result in another flush of gorgeous blossoms. As always, you have the choice of tossing the plant out and starting over again with a new tuber or specimen. You may be pleasantly surprised if you try to carry the gloxinia over.

Forcing a Rest: Once flowers have faded and there are no unopened buds tucked under the foliage, cut off all top growth as close to the tuber as possible — even if the leaves are still green. You may find tiny new shoots just emerging from the tuber. If so, leave them alone — they are the beginning of a new flush of growth.

Repotting and Soil Mixture: After the top growth has been removed, carefully repot the leafless tuber in an azalea pan, a clay container available from garden centers that is wider and shorter than a standard pot. Don't worry if the original pot was not an azalea pan. The new container should be only ½ inch larger in diameter than the old one. Place clay shards over the drainage holes in the bottom of the pot to prevent them from clogging with soil.

When repotting, try not to disturb the roots, which are still functioning. Repot at a depth that will leave the top of the tuber even with the soil surface, not buried underground. A potting mix of 2 parts peat moss, 1 part packaged potting soil, and 1 part perlite is ideal. Gloxinia tubers sprout in about 8 weeks, though this varies considerably depending on variety and environmental conditions.

Light, Temperature, Moisture, and Fertilizer: Provide the newly potted tuber with the same amount of light you would a full-grown specimen — either 4 hours of very bright indirect light or 12 to 14 hours of artificial light each day.

Water the newly scalped tuber only when the top *half* of soil in the pan feels totally dry. Then irrigate thoroughly, until water runs through the drainage holes in the bottom of the pot. Once a new growth begins, set plants on a pebble tray to increase humidity. Start watering when the top layer of soil in the pot feels dry. Provide the same temperatures as recommended under "Cultural Requirements," above.

HYDRANGEA

Do not begin fertilizing until new growth appears. Then fertilize every 2 weeks with a water-soluble chemical product recommended for use on houseplants, at one-half the strength suggested on the label. Once the leaves have grown above the pot's rim, fertilize every 2 weeks at full strength.

Soon you will have a magnificent specimen full of flowers, and you can follow the same instructions for its care as provided under "Cultural Requirements," above. Carrying a gloxinia over for more than 3 years is not recommended, as they become less productive after that amount of time.

Pruning: Often, more than one shoot grows from a single gloxinia tuber. All but the strongest one should be cut off as close to the tuber as possible while they are still very small.

HYDRANGEA

Hydrangeas have lavish flowers, luscious colors, and excellent indoor-keeping qualities. Their enormous snowball-like blossoms are a familiar sight in florist shops and garden centers during the spring and early summer. The fabulous blooms last and last, making the plant an excellent gift.

The bigleaf or house hydrangea *(Hydrangea macrophylla)* is well known as a potted plant, but even better known and more widely grown as a shrub, particularly in the South and along coastal areas.

Planted in the open soil, the bigleaf hydrangea generally reaches a height of 4 to 6 feet. Potted flowering specimens are usually in the 18- to 24-inch range. Colors include white, as well as shades of pink, red, blue, and mauve, and combinations of these hues, depending on which of the approximately 50 varieties is being grown.

The flower color of bigleaf hydrangeas depends not only on the variety grown, but also on the level of acidity in the soil, a factor known as soil pH. For the most part, hydrangea flowers are blue if the soil is acid and pink if the soil is alkaline. The white-flowered types are an exception; they remain white regardless of soil conditions.

CULTURAL REQUIREMENTS

You have only to meet a few simple requirements to keep the flowers on your newly acquired hydrangea fresh for several weeks. Even the eventual decline of the blooms is accompanied by an appealing softening of their color, a phenomenon which prolongs the period of enjoyment.

SELECTION

When shopping for a hydrangea, look for healthy, rich, green foliage and fresh, clear-colored blossoms. Also keep an eye out for the following problems:

- Yellowing of the leaves between the veins may be caused by an iron deficiency, poor root growth, an inadequate nitrogen supply, or overly alkaline soil.

- The absence of lower leaves is often the result of overcrowding, pest damage, or a moisture imbalance.

- A cottony fungal growth on the leaves, called "powdery mildew," is a common hydrangea malady. It often is caused by a combination of cool nights and poor air circulation around plants during the growing period.

- Spider mites, aphids, and cyclamen mites are other pests to be aware of.

Light: Provide bright indirect light such as that found in front of an unobstructed northern window. Too much light may cause flowers to droop.

Temperature: Night temperatures of 55° to 60° F. and day temperatures of 68°-72° F. are ideal for prolonging flower freshness.

Moisture: Hydrangeas require lots of water. You will find that

41

the top layer of soil in the container dries unusually fast between waterings. It is important to feel the soil daily. When the top layer is dry, water thoroughly, until water runs through the drainage holes in the bottom of the container.

Plant Care After Flowers Fade

After the hydrangea flowers have faded, the plant should be cut back to about 1 inch above the old growth. You can distinguish between old and new growth because the young wood is green and the old wood is brown. Such pruning is essential to the production of new growth on which flowers will form.

Availability

Potted flowering hydrangeas are most abundant during the spring. As a consequence, they are closely associated with Easter and Mother's Day gift-giving.

Where the climate permits, in parts of Zone 5 and southward, hydrangeas can be planted permanently in the garden; subsequent blooms inside the home will not nearly match the possibilities outside. In northern parts of Zone 5 and northward, hydrangeas cannot tolerate the low winter temperatures and must be brought back indoors after the first autumn frost.

The Hydrangea Outdoors

Select a well-drained site for planting. If the soil has a high clay content (easily detected by its red color and sticky feel), dig in some organic matter such as compost or peat moss to improve the texture. Choose a spot that will allow the shrub to reach its potential size. Hydrangeas grow quickly to 6 feet in height *and* width — 12 feet if undamaged by low winter temperatures and left unpruned. If you live as far north as Zone 6, choose a protected spot, such as near the house or behind a windbreak, that still meets the plant's light requirements.

The best-flowering specimens are grown in full sun, though hydrangeas tolerate and also flower well in light shade.

The hydrangea should be deeply watered during dry periods, especially the first year after planting, when its roots are not well established.

If you have planted your hydrangea where the soil is high in nutrients, you will probably not need to fertilize. Otherwise, you should apply a dry slow-release fertilizer in early spring when growth begins, or supply a liquid feed throughout the growing season.

Shrubs planted outdoors should be pruned in very early spring, before new growth begins. Cut back shoots that flowered the previous summer to within two pairs of buds from ground level. (The spent blossoms will probably have remained throughout winter, so you will have no trouble determining which branches have bloomed.) Also, cut out weak stems and any frost-damaged wood. Neglected plants soon become stubby and unattractive. Old plants in need of rejuvenation can be sheared to ground level in early spring, resulting in dramatically improved specimens within a few years.

Setting the Hydrangea Out for the Summer

In colder parts of Zone 5 and northward, after the pruning that follows the indoor-blooming period, repot the hydrangea in a container about 2 inches larger than the original one. Equal parts packaged potting soil, peat moss, and perlite make a suitable growing medium.

Place the newly potted plant in a sunny part of the garden after danger of frost has passed. To avoid wind damage, sink the pot up to its rim in the soil. Remember that hydrangeas require frequent watering, especially when temperatures are high, so check the potting soil often.

After the first hard autumn frost, bring the plant into a cold but frost-free cellar or garage and leave it there. Water the hydrangea often enough to keep the soil moist, until around the first week of February. It is important that the existing stems do not die

PRIMROSE

during this period, because they are bearing next summer's flower buds. Hydrangeas bloom on old wood, not new growth.

After the first week in February, bring the plant into a sunny room that is about 50° F. at night for about 3 weeks. Then move it to a spot where temperatures are in the 65° to 70° F. range, and set it on a sunny windowsill. Continue to water freely when the top layer of soil feels dry to the touch. Once the plant is in bloom, provide the same care as described under "Cultural Requirements" above.

Primrose

Primroses are sold not only as garden plants, but also as potted specimens for holiday giving. The popular polyantha type bears flowers in a wonderfully wide range of colors, either solid or variegated, including white, yellow, pink, red, rose, apricot, lavender, and purple. Flowers are about 2 inches across and are produced on 6- to 12-inch stalks above the foliage. The rough-textured leaves, about 1 foot long, are produced in a low-growing rosette. This plant blooms naturally in May, but is forced by the professionals to flower during Easter and before. The polyantha primrose is a perennial, hardy in zones 3 to 8, where it can be permanently planted outdoors after its flowers fade.

The fairy primrose *(Primula malacoides)* is another of the more popular species. It bears tufts of flowers less than 1 inch across, in white and shades of pink, red, or lilac, held above the foliage on plants up to 1½ feet high. Its long-stalked, oval leaves are about 3 inches long. The fairy primrose is an annual plant raised in commercial greenhouses for winter and spring sales. It is generally discarded after the flowering period.

SELECTION

Select a healthy-looking plant with green leaves; yellowing of the foliage indicates overly acid soil, overwatering, a fertilizer imbalance, or pesticide damage. Make sure there are plenty of flowers yet to open after purchase. Watch out for leaf spots, indicating one of various fungi, and a mosaic pattern on the foliage, indicating viral infection. Also, keep an eye out for aphids, mealybugs, and spider mites.

CULTURAL REQUIREMENTS

Light: Bright indirect light is recommended. Placement on a northern windowsill or in front of a sunnier window where light is diffused by sheer curtains, partially closed shutters, or shrubs growing in front of the window should do nicely.

Temperature: Night temperatures of 40° to 50° F. and day temperatures of 68° F. or lower are ideal. Primroses may decline rapidly if temperatures are too high.

Moisture: Water thoroughly when the top soil layer in the container feels dry to the touch. Wait about 15 minutes and discard the excess moisture that accumulates in the drip plate beneath the pot.

AVAILABILITY

Primroses are found in shops from around the first of the year through early spring. Those that flower closer to their natural time — around Easter — seem to adjust more readily to life indoors and generally hold up longer.

After the flowers of the fairy primroses fade, the plants should be discarded. The polyantha primrose is another matter. If you live in zones 3 to 8, the plant can be set out in the garden as a permanent part of your collection. Its bright floral colors will make a wonderful addition to the early spring garden, complementing the spring flowering bulbs beautifully.

Sometime after the ground has thawed in spring, select a moist, well-drained spot in a partially shaded area. Dig some leaf mold into the soil. Unpot and plant the primrose at approximately the same depth at which it was set in its container. Mulch the primrose after planting to keep the soil cool and moist. Remulch before winter to protect it from the elements.

Chapter 4
Summer Plants

Anthurium

The strangely beautiful blooms of anthuriums are composed of a waxy leaflike structure called a *spathe,* 3 to 5 inches wide and about 6 inches long, which supports a yellow column called a *spadix.* The spathe may be the brightest red or orange imagin-

able, a clear pink or white, or multicolored. The spadix is actually made up of hundreds of tiny flowers, some male, others female — though the difference is not discernible with the naked eye. They are usually straight, but one fairly common species, *Anthurium scherzerianum,* bears a spadix curled like a pig's tail. Anthurium blooms last for weeks, whether left on the plant or removed for use as cut flowers. *Anthurium andreanum,* the most commonly grown species, reaches a height of about 3 feet. *Anthurium scherzeria-*

ANTHURIUM

num is less than 12 inches tall

Availability and Selection

Anthurium plants may be more difficult to come by than many other flowering houseplants, though a trip through the plant businesses in your town, via the yellow pages, should reveal a source at almost any season. Large specimens are dearly priced. For economy's sake you may wish to go with a young plant.

Large and small plants are generally sold in bloom. Do not settle for one that does not have at least one flower bud. Look for healthy green leaves, free of any black, yellow, or brown spots, and a compact, upright specimen..

Cultural Requirements

Anthuriums require very bright indirect light. An east-facing window that gets the morning sun is perfect. A south-facing window where strong sun is obstructed by trees or neighboring buildings will also do nicely. A western exposure will suffice as long as plants are protected from the hot after-noon rays in summer; you can close sheer curtains or move plants back several feet from the window. Too much light may result in scorched foliage on the portion of the plant closest to the window. Too little light may mean an absence of flowers, spindly growth, and plants that require staking to stay upright.

Night temperatures of 60° to 65° F. and day temperatures of 65° F. or higher are perfect for anthuriums.

Water these plants thoroughly when the top layer of potting mix feels dry to the touch. Since anthuriums thrive in a moist, tropical environment, supply constant humidity through the use of a pebble tray.

Fertilize monthly at the full strength recommended on the label with a water-soluble chemical fertilizer high in phosphorus, such as a product with an analysis of 15-30-15. Omit fertilizer from Christmas through mid-March, while plants are not actively growing.

Many growers recommend a potting mixture of 2 parts fine grade fir bark plus 1 part coarse peat moss. This mix is great, but fir bark may be hard to come by. If you do not have access to this product, use a mix of 2 parts packaged potting soil to 1 part perlite.

FUCHSIA

Clay pots are recommended for anthuriums because they cause the soil to dry out more quickly between waterings, which is perfect for these plants. When repotting, use a container 1 inch larger in diameter than the old one.

Anthuriums do not require pruning. If the plant becomes too large for the space in which it is growing, you can cut back the stem to keep it within bounds, and the plant will fare well.

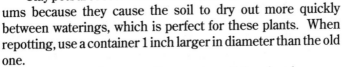

FUCHSIA

With glorious cascades of delicate, often multicolored blossoms, pots of hanging fuchsia are one of the most elegant of summer flowers.

Fuchsia is named for Leonard Fuchs, who lived in the first half of the sixteenth century. The genus *Fuchsia* includes more than 50 species.

DESCRIPTION

Fuchsias have blossoms in a variety of reds, pinks, and purples. Those with bicolored blossoms, most often purple and pink or pink and white, are the most stunning, unusual, and popular. Fuchsia plants bloom throughout the summer. If they are to be carried over, they require a period of cold and dormancy during the winter months.

Cultural Requirements During the Blooming Period

Light: Bright, indirect light is best for fuchsias. They should be protected both from intense sun and strong winds. The hotter your area, the more your fuchsia should be protected from direct sun.

Moisture: Fuchsia thrives with frequent, light waterings. Water when the top layer of soil feels dry to the touch. In the height of summer heat, they often need light watering twice a day, in the morning and evening. When it is very hot, a spray mist of water will help keep fuchsias in good shape.

Fertilizer: Fuchsia should be fed in small, regular doses, with a low nitrogen fertilizer. Follow package directions with care.

Pruning: There is no need to prune the fuchsia during the blooming period, but spent blossoms should be removed immediately to ensure continuous blooming.

Plant Care After the Blooming Period

Many people throw out their fuchsias at the end of summer. This is the only viable option for those who cannot give these plants the cold environment they need for wintering over. If you have a basement or other place to winter over your fuchsias, though, it's worth giving it a try.

Before the first frost, cut the plant back to the soil and put it, pot and all, in a basement or other dark area where the temperature is about 40° F.

Plants should be kept rather dry during this period. Water when the top half of the soil has completely dried out, and only enough to moisturize all the soil again.

In late winter or early spring — sometime in February or March — repot the fuchsia in a mixture of loam, sand, bone-

AVAILABILITY AND SELECTION

Fuchsias are available at garden centers in most sections of the country from May through July.

Select a plant with dark green, healthy-looking foliage. The plant chosen should have blossoms in various stages of development, from buds to full bloom. Fortunately, fuchsias have few pests, so this is less likely to be a problem than with other flowering houseplants. Nevertheless, they are not immune from pests or diseases. Look over the chosen specimen carefully.

Full-page photo: Pocketbook plant (*Calceolaria crenatifolia*). ANN REILLY: PHOTO/NATS. **Inset: Azalea as a container plant.** JERRY HOWARD/POSITIVE IMAGES.

Full-page photo: Forced paperwhite narcissus.
JERRY HOWARD/POSITIVE IMAGES. **Inset, top: Pink
hyacinths (Hyacinthus orientalis).** MAGGIE OSTER.
Inset, above: Red tulips (Tulipa hybrid). MAGGIE
OSTER.

Full-page photo: Assorted African violets (*Saintpaulia* hybrid). MAGGIE OSTER. **Inset: Kalanchoe *(Kalanchoe pumila).*** DAVID M. STONE: PHOTO/NATS.

Full-page photo: Red anthurium. JERRY HOWARD/
POSITIVE IMAGES. **Inset: Yellow primrose and
assorted cineraria.** MADELAINE GRAY.

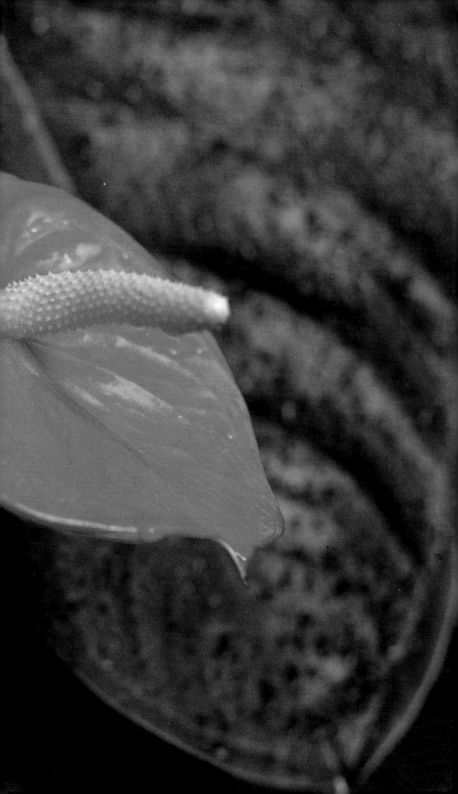

Full-page photo: Rieger begonia, 'Whisper o'Pink' (*Begonia* x *hiemalis*). ANN REILLY: PHOTO/ NATS. **Inset:** *Hydrangea macrophylla.* ANN REILLY: PHOTO/NATS.

meal, and leaf mold, all of which are available from garden-supply centers.

Begin following the same cultural requirements as for blooming fuchsias.

As new shoots appear, it is essential to pinch them back to make a compact, dense plant. Continue pinching back shoots until a good base has formed and pinch thereafter until the plant has reached the right proportions.

GARDENIA

A rich and often-imitated floral scent as well as leaves with the highest glossy shine make the gardenia a wonderful plant. However, gardenias are fussy, unpredictable, and have a penchant for unpleasant problems. The gardenia is like a thoroughbred — it requires constant and doting care to perform to its full potential, but when that potential is reached, the plant has almost no equal.

DESCRIPTION

Waxy white flowers, potentially 3 or more inches across, and a strong, sweet scent are the trademarks of the gardenia.

Gardenia blossoms may be born year-round, though spring blooming is the most prolific. Like the blossoms of many other white-flowered plants, gardenia petals turn brown all too soon. Generally, this has nothing to do with inept care. It is just the way of gardenias, though touching the blossoms may hasten discoloration.

GARDENIA

AVAILABILITY

Plant shops and garden centers may offer gardenias at any time of year, though they are generally more plentiful around Christmas, Valentine's Day, Easter, and Mother's Day. Plants purchased during these holidays are usually loaded with flower buds about to open. Commercial growers achieve this enticing and obviously saleable state by subjecting the plants to high temperatures around the clock to encourage rapid growth. Then they turn the thermostat down to about 60° F. at night to promote flower bud formation. In a short while the plants are ready for the marketplace.

Light: The gardenia requires at least 4 hours of direct light each day. Do not worry about too much summer sun. Gardenias can thrive and flower beautifully when grown in containers placed outdoors on a patio in full sun. As long as high light intensity is compensated for with ample moisture, success is yours. Maximum light is particularly important during the winter, when dull and cloudy days are the norm.

Temperature: For continuous flowering, provide night temperatures of 60° F. Night temperatures above 65° F. will probably

Selection

With gardenias, the season of purchase makes little difference, and whether your plant is bought with a multitude of flower buds about to burst open or just a few will soon be irrelevant. After a time the plant will adjust to conditions in your home, and with proper care it may bloom intermittently through most of the year.

When shopping for a gardenia, pay less attention to the number of buds than to general health and appearance. You want a well-branched, vigorous specimen that is pest-free.

Gardenias are particularly prone to mealybugs. Spider mites and soft scale insects also frequent the gardenia. They are also susceptible to a fungus disease called stem cankers. Damage is frequently found at the point where the stem meets the soil line. The cankers look like sores or lesions overgrown with corky tissue which radiates from the canker. Also avoid plants with discolored spots, blotches, or dead patches on the foliage.

inhibit flower bud formation. Day temperatures of 68° to 75° F. are ideal. Of course, day temperatures will go higher during the summer, but if you water as needed, all will be well.

Moisture: For gardenias, the soil should be kept constantly and evenly moist, but never soggy. Water thoroughly when the top layer of soil begins to feel dry to the touch. Plants kept too wet or too dry are likely to lose the lower older leaves as well as flower buds.

High humidity, a requirement too often unfulfilled, is also essential to successful gardenia care. The use of a humidifying pebble tray (as described on page 6) is a must for all gardenias grown outside the tropics.

Fertilizer: If a plant could have an appetite, the gardenia would be ravenous. It must have regular fertilization with a granular chemical fertilizer recommended for use on acid-loving plants.

Monthly applications at the full strength suggested on the label are fine, but application every other week at half strength is even better, since a more continuous source of nutrients is provided.

Gardenias frequently suffer from chlorosis, a fancy word for yellow leaves. Chlorosis is often evidenced by areas between the leaf veins turning yellow, while veined areas stay green. Chlorosis is often caused by an iron deficiency and can be easily remedied by the application of chelated iron. This product is mixed with water and either poured into the soil or sprayed on the foliage; follow the label instructions. Applying iron chelate 3 or 4 times a year may help prevent chlorosis altogether.

Placement in the Home: To provide ample light, you will probably have to place the gardenia in front of the sunniest window in your home. Avoid drafty areas such as those near a door that is frequently opened or near a heating or air-conditioning vent. The gardenia may react to drafts by dropping leaves and flower buds.

Gardenias flourish outdoors during the summer, especially in humid climates. Place them in a spot that gets the morning sun but is protected from the hot afternoon rays. They will do well in the hot afternoon sun, but the need for watering may be too great to suit your schedule. While the plant is outside, check it daily to see if watering is needed and continue to fertilize regularly. Be sure to bring your plant back inside before there's a danger of frost.

Flower Bud Drop: The most common cause of complaint among gardenia owners is flower bud drop. It is depressing to anxiously await the opening of the lovely blossoms only to have them thwart you by dropping early. This is almost always caused by a failure to follow one of the cultural practices required, especially those of high humidity and ample light intensity.

Potting and Soil: Gardenias need repotting when roots start growing out of the drainage holes, when the soil dries out unusually fast between waterings, or when the water runs through the potting mix faster than in the past. Select a new container that is 1 to 1½ inches larger in diameter and height than the old one. An ideal soil mix consists of 1 part packaged potting soil, 1 part perlite, and 2 parts peat moss. This mix drains beautifully, is acid enough for gardenias, and contains ample organic matter.

Pruning: In the spring, before new growth commences, prune and shape gardenia plants, removing any overgrown shoots or overcrowded branches. Then snip off the ends of each stem to encourage a flush of new growth. Spindly plants that have been blooming poorly and are in need of complete rejuvenation should be pruned back to a height of 6 inches during early spring. Faded flowers should be removed promptly by cutting them off just above a node, the point where a leaf joins the stem.

To produce a few large flowers instead of many smaller ones, remove all but one flower bud from each stem.

ORCHIDS

Many people believe that plants capable of producing such exquisite blossoms as orchids are beyond the horticultural capabilities of amateur gardeners. While some orchids are difficult to bring into flower (indeed, even tricky to keep alive), there are beautiful orchids that make wonderful windowsill plants and demand no more care than a gardenia.

DESCRIPTION

The orchid family is one of the largest in the plant kingdom, with approximately 30,000 species and countless hybrids. It is also one of the most diverse groups in habit of growth, variety of color, flower shape and size, and fragrance.

ORCHID

Three extraordinarily beautiful, popular, and widely available orchid genera (groups of plants with similar floral characteristics) that can be successfully grown and brought into bloom by the dedicated novice are *Cattleya, Paphiopedilum,* and *Phalaenopsis.* All three are frequently recommended for beginners, yet are found in the collections of the most sophisticated hobbyists and professionals as well.

Cattleya orchids (or "cats," as they are called for short) are among the showiest orchid flowers. The colors are as varied as the spectrum of a rainbow. Uncommonly rich yellows, lavenders, mixtures of colors, white, pink, and even reds provide all the beauty you could ask for in a flower. *Cattleya*s have 3 petals. The lower petal, known as the *lip* or *labellum,* is the largest, showiest, and most colorfully marked. Set slightly behind the petals are 3 sepals, which resemble and are colored like petals but are generally narrower. The flowers are usually 3 to 5 inches long and often appear on plants about 2 feet high (though species with much smaller flowers do exist). Most *Cattleya*s bear 1 to 7 blossoms once each year. The flowering season and the fragrance depend on which variety is grown, but all flowers are long-lasting unless temperatures are uncommonly high.

*Cattleya*s produce multiple vertical stems, known as *pseudobulbs,* which grow from a horizontal ground stem. In cultivation, the ground stem creeps along the surface of the potting medium. Flowers are formed at the leaf bases on the newest pseudobulbs. The nonflowering stems are called *backbulbs.*

Paphiopedilum orchids, commonly called lady's slippers, are named for their lowermost petal, the lip, which forms a slipperlike pouch. The other two petals are narrower and frequently spotted. They may also bear hair- or molelike appendages — characteristics that only enhance their strange beauty. *Paphiopedilum*s, like *Cattleya*s, have 3 sepals, the uppermost of which is known as the *dorsal sepal.* It may be larger than the other two and is usually the most beautifully colored. *Paphiopedilum* flower colors include white, green, yellow, pink, brown, and every combination of those hues. They bloom once a year, but the flowers may last for weeks, and large multiflowered specimens may stay in bloom for months. Species vary considerably in size, though plants are usually about 1 foot high and flowers 3 to 5 inches long.

The leaves are arranged in 2 rows, and flowers emerge singly from down in the center of the leaves. There are hundreds of hybrids, but those with mottled or spotted foliage, as opposed to solid green leaves, make easier houseplants.

Phalaenopsis orchids are called "moth orchids" because their flowers supposedly resemble moths in flight. Colors include white and shades of pink, yellow, and purple, with many striped and spotted varieties among the multitude of hybrids. Several flowers are born simultaneously on a gracefully arching flower stalk, 2 to 4 feet long, that emerges from the center of the plant. Moth orchids produce a handful of strap-shaped leaves, about 1 foot long. They usually bloom once a year, generally in spring, but if the flower stalk is cut back after flowers have faded, a second set of blossoms may develop.

Cultural Requirements

Of the three orchid genera described, the *Paphiopedilum*s are the easiest to grow. Their blossoms, which last for weeks, are among the most strange and beautiful flowers in the world. The *Phalaenopsis* orchids are the second easiest to maintain.

Their blossoms are also long-lasting. The *Cattleya*s seem to be the most difficult of the three to bring into bloom, probably because they require such high light intensity.

Light: *Paphiopedilum* and *Phalaenopsis* orchids should be placed in front of a very bright, unobstructed window. Trees growing in front of the window, drawn curtains, or nearby buildings can block out light and prevent blossoming. To prevent foliage burn

SELECTION

Orchids are relatively expensive, although young plants may be priced under $10, especially if they have not yet flowered. Well-established blooming specimens can be very costly. It is worthwhile to shop around and compare prices as well as stock. If you are faced with a stand filled with orchids—a rare situation indeed—here are a few tips to help in your selection:

■ If affordable, buy a plant in bloom. Orchids usually bloom once a year, and, if the plant is out of flower, you cannot be sure when it bloomed last or when it will bloom again.

■ Orchids are subject to several viral diseases, which cause yellow mosaiclike patterns, yellow spots, and blotches on the leaves, and a streaked, water-stained appearance on the flowers. Check the leaves and flowers carefully.

■ Orchids are usually grown in a potting mixture that contains fir bark chips or tree fern fiber. The medium should look fresh and should not be broken down or decomposed—indications that the plant has needed repotting for too long.

■ The newest leaves on the plant should be as large as the older leaves. If they are larger, all the better. This suggests that the current year's growth was made under proper growing conditions.

■ The flowers should be firm, fresh, and waxy in appearance — not flaccid, faded, or washed-out.

■ Purchase orchids from a reputable dealer, preferably one that knows about orchids and can help you with a selection. The better shops may guarantee your new orchid for a reasonable period of time.

during summer, close sheer curtains, partially close Venetian blinds, or move plants back from the window a few feet.

*Cattleya*s require more light than *Paphiopedilum* or *Phalaenopsis* orchids and grow best in front of an unobstructed south-facing window. It is said that a good test for ensuring that *Cattleya*s receive adequate light is to determine whether there is enough light to take a photograph with an instamatic camera without a flash. If so, there is sufficient light to grow a *Cattleya* orchid.

Temperature: *Cattleya, Paphiopedilum,* and *Phalaenopsis* orchids will do well and flower predictably when day temperatures are 65° to 75° F. and there is a 5 to 10 degree drop in night temperature. If plants are grown near a window, they will probably experience this drop in night temperature due to loss of heat through the glass.

Moisture: Water orchids when the growing medium feels dry to the touch; then soak thoroughly. Since orchids are grown in a fast-draining material, you need to pour about 3 times as much water into the container as you would for other plants in comparably sized pots to be sure of adequately moistening the medium. With the potting materials used for orchids, you must move the spout of your watering can all over the surface of the growing medium to be sure it is soaked thoroughly. An orchid mix should not be kept constantly wet, nor should it be allowed to dry completely. Since many disease organisms thrive in a moist, dark environment, most growers water in the morning so that moisture evaporates before evening. Tepid water is recommended.

Slightly reduce the frequency with which you water *Paphiopedilum* and *Phalaenopsis* orchids while they are in flower. Reduce the frequency with *Cattleya*s when new leaves have reached the size of mature leaves. Resume watering *Cattleya*s as before when new growth appears.

AVAILABILITY

Orchids are available throughout the year. They are not sold in most plant shops, however; you will probably have to call the larger florist shops and garden centers to check on available stock. Even the most diversified plant businesses are unlikely to carry a wide orchid selection. Some specialty growers, though, carry more types of *Cattleya, Paphiopedilum,* and *Phalaenopsis* orchids than you can imagine.

All three genera described here require a relative humidity of 46 to 60 percent, more moist than most homes. An easy way to increase humidity is to place plants on a watertight tray filled with small damp pebbles as described on page 6.

Syringing or misting plants also increases humidity, though only for a short time. Syringing is not a substitute for the pebble tray, but it can be a supplement. To help prevent disease, always syringe orchids on sunny days, so that the leaves do not stay damp too long, and mist plants early in the day so moisture will evaporate by evening. Never spray plants directly at close range. Instead, spray the area around the plants so that a fine mist settles on the foliage.

Fertilizer: Orchids growing in a mixture that includes fir bark chips should be fertilized with a water-soluble chemical fertilizer labeled 30-10-10. Apply fertilizer at the strength recommended on the label once a month — or, better yet, at half strength every 2 weeks, for a more continuous nutrient supply. Orchids grown in a mix containing tree fern fiber should be fertilized with a balanced chemical fertilizer, such as a product with an analysis of 20-20-20, every month at full strength or every 2 weeks at half strength.

Potting and Soil: Most professional growers use a mix based on fir tree bark chips ("fir bark") or the fiber from the stalks of Mexican tree ferns ("tree fern fiber"). Either of these materials is mixed with a coarse grade of peat moss. You will do just fine by potting *Cattleya* and *Phalaenopsis* orchids in 2 parts fir bark or tree fern fiber and 1 part coarse peat moss.

It is necessary to repot orchids when the plant itself, not just the roots, starts growing over the edge of the pot. Do not repot *Cattleya* and *Phalaenopsis* orchids until you see new roots growing. If it is necessary to repot *Paphiopedilum*s, wait until right after they have finished blooming.

Always repot into a container large enough to accommodate 2 years' growth. To repot, tap the plant out of its pot and remove the old growing medium from around the roots. Trim off any dead roots with a knife that you have sterilized by passing through a flame.

Orchids are repotted differently from other houseplants. Only *Phalaenopsis* orchids are centered in the container, because they grow up, not across. *Cattleya*s and *Paphiopedilum*s grow across; they should be repotted so that the oldest part of the plant is against one side of the pot and there is ample room between it and the opposite pot wall. New growth will fill in this area.

Place broken clay shards over the drainage holes of an adequately sized clay or plastic pot. Most orchid fanciers prefer clay for its natural appearance, fast drainage, and the fact that clay "breathes" — allowing an exchange of air with the outside environment. Fill the pot halfway to the top with one of the mixes recommended. Hold the plant over the pot so the tops of the roots are just below the pot rim. Fill in around the roots with the medium, packing it tightly. After repotting, water thoroughly. Mist plants twice daily for a week or so after potting. Orchids may require staking to stay upright.

Pruning: Orchids are pruned to remove spent flowers and leaves that have turned yellow. Again, make all cuts with a sterile knife. After the blossoms have faded, *Phalaenopsis* flower stalks can be cut just below where the flowers developed to promote a second flowering — a special bonus with this group. The flowers of all other orchids are removed along with their stalks.

CHAPTER 5

AUTUMN PLANTS

AMARYLLIS

If your list of desirable traits in flowering houseplants starts with drama and ends with subtlety, the amaryllis should suit you to a tee.

DESCRIPTION

The amaryllis is considered a "tender bulb." It will not survive winters outdoors except in Zone 9. Generally speaking, if you live anywhere other than Florida or southern California the amaryllis is strictly a houseplant.

Amaryllis flower colors include white, various pinks and lavenders, shades of red (including some of the richest reds imaginable), and several extraordinary bicolors — red and white among the showiest. The trumpet-shaped blossoms, usually 4 to 8 inches wide, have 5 petals and are produced in a group of 4 (though sometimes only 2 or 3 blossoms appear simultaneously) on thick stems about 2 feet high. The *anthers,* threadlike structures produced in the center of the flower, bear bright yellow pollen, which contrasts strikingly with the petal color.

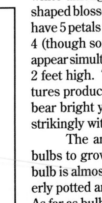

AMARYLLIS

The amaryllis is among the easiest bulbs to grow. In fact, a newly purchased bulb is almost guaranteed to bloom if properly potted and provided with a few basics. As far as bulbs are concerned, it is about as foolproof as you can get.

An amaryllis bulb can be frightfully expensive, up to $25 per bulb — much more than a hyacinth or a handful of daffodils. But the plant can be forced to bloom again and again with a minimum of effort.

AVAILABILITY AND SELECTION

Amaryllis bulbs are generally available in garden centers from October through December. They bloom about 8 weeks after planting. The amaryllis bulb increases in size each season, so you can, in essence, grow your own giant-sized bulb in due course. As with other bulbs, select a specimen that is firm all over, with no soft or rotten spots.

Many of the bulbs offered for sale have already started producing leaves or a flower bud. If the growth has just begun, you have a little head start. However, if growth is several inches high, pick another bulb. An amaryllis which has grown that much before planting has been forced to live off the moisture and nutrients stored inside the bulb — not a good situation.

Cultural Requirements

There is nothing tricky about planting an amaryllis bulb and getting it to bloom. The challenge is in carrying the bulb over and persuading it to flower the following year. Even this task is not really difficult and no special equipment or conditions are needed. It is just a bit time-consuming and requires some perseverance.

Planting the Bulb: Place a clay shard or a small piece of wire screening over the drainage hole of a pot that is 1½ to 2 inches larger in diameter than the widest part of the bulb. The pot may seem a bit snug, but amaryllis grow s best in tight containers.

Prepare a growing medium of 2 parts packaged potting soil, 1 part perlite, and approximately 1 tablespoon of a slow-release pellet fertilizer recommended for use on flowering houseplants. The fertilizer will help supply the nutrients necessary for the production of next year's blossoms.

Pot the bulb, pointed-end up, so that the top half is above the soil line and the bottom half is below ground. This may seem odd, but bulbs planted this way seem to flower more freely. After potting, water thoroughly, until water runs through the drainage holes in the bottom of the pot.

Plant Care After Planting: Place the newly potted bulb on a sunny windowsill in a room where temperatures range between 55° F. and 65° F. Warmer temperatures may result in growth that is weak and floppy. While flowers will still be produced, staking may be required. Cooler temperatures result in sturdier growth.

Water thoroughly whenever the top layer of soil feels dry to the touch. If the soil is kept too wet, the bulb may rot — a constant threat with bulbous plants. As the roots develop and fill the container, the top layer of soil will dry out more quickly and the frequency of watering should be increased accordingly.

Leaves may develop first, or the bud may emerge from the side of the bulb before the appearance of foliage. Once growth begins, give the pot a quarter turn every few days to prevent the plant from leaning toward the light.

Remove the flowers after they have opened and faded, but do not cut off the green flower stalk or any of the foliage. Place the plant back on a sunny windowsill. Continue to water thoroughly when the top layer of soil feels dry to the touch. Frequently, the bulb will send up a second set of blossoms — most likely if you are growing one of the larger bulbs. The second set of flowers may be smaller than the first.

Before you know whether the second flower set will arrive or not, begin fertilizing with a water-soluble chemical fertilizer recommended for use on flowering houseplants. Fertilize every month at the strength recommended on the label. This will help supply the bulb with the nutrients needed to produce next year's flowers.

You must then continue to treat the amaryllis as if it were any other houseplant with regard to light, water, and fertilizer, until the foliage and the flower stalk yellow naturally. This means keeping it on a sunny windowsill, watering thoroughly when the top layer of soil feels dry to the touch, and fertilizing monthly. If the plant is neglected and allowed to decline prematurely, it may not flower again.

Some folks place the potted amaryllis outdoors during the spring, after the danger of frost has passed. One of the main advantages of this is the removal of the declining amaryllis from the windowsill. Plants set outdoors should be placed where they receive sunlight in the morning and partial shade during the afternoon. While the plant is outdoors, check often to see if watering is needed and continue to fertilize as before until the foliage yellows.

Plant Care After the Foliage Yellows: The foliage and flower stalk of your amaryllis will stay green throughout the spring and will probably turn yellow during the summer or early autumn. This depends on the hybrid grown and on your particular conditions. At any rate, once the leaves have yellowed, remove them just above the tip of the bulb. Then store the potted bulb in a place where it will be out of sight but not forgotten. A cool place (55° to 65° F.) such as a basement or a closet that backs onto an outside wall will do perfectly. Just do the best you can to provide such low temperatures during the height of summer.

If the amaryllis was outside in the summer, bring it back indoors before the first frost. If the foliage has yellowed, remove it and store the potted bulb in a cool place. If the leaves are still green, place it on a sunny windowsill and provide the same care as before until yellowing occurs.

Forcing a Second Flowering

The amaryllis requires a 3- to 4-month period of cool and dry conditioning between the time the foliage yellows and the time you begin the process of forcing it to bloom again.

Once the cool, dry period has passed, take the potted bulb out of hiding and carefully scrape off the top 1 to 2 inches of soil. Replace the top of the old medium with fresh mix. Amaryllis do best when their roots are left undisturbed. When repotting, choose a container 1½ to 2 inches larger in diameter than the widest part of the bulb, which will by now have increased in size.

Water thoroughly. Then place the potted bulb on a sunny windowsill and follow the instructions given under "Plant Care After Planting," above.

Aphelandra

The aphelandra is nicknamed "zebra plant" for its pointed oval leaves, up to 12 inches long, which are rich green and boldly striped white. Leaves are produced on stems up to 3 feet high, though most windowsill subjects are in the 1- to 2-foot range. Very large spikes of bright yellow flowers normally appear each fall, though plants bloom at other seasons as well.

The major problem with this plant is that it drops lower leaves no matter how well it's tended. Increased humidity helps slow this irritating occurrence, but does not prevent it. Eventually, you wind up with a bare-legged specimen topped with a cluster of leaves.

APHELANDRA

Cultural Requirements

There is nothing difficult about aphelandra culture, unless you count the minor nuisance of filling a pebble tray with water to keep the environment around the plant adequately humid. Otherwise, with simple care you get a lovely flower show each fall and a striking foliage display year-round.

Light, Temperature, and Moisture: Supply the aphelandra with very bright indirect light, exactly as described for anthuriums on pp. 46-47. Night temperatures of 60° to 65° F. and day temperatures of 65° F. or above are ideal. Water the aphelandra thoroughly when the top layer of soil feels dry to the touch. Wait about 15 minutes and discard any excess moisture that has accumulated in the drip plate beneath the container. Check the aphelandra often to see if watering is needed. Provide a pebble tray and be sure it is properly filled at all times.

Fertilizer: Apply a water-soluble chemical fertilizer each month as recommended on the label. A product with an analysis of 15-30-15 is ideal. Do not fertilize from Christmas through mid-March.

Placement in the Home: Place the aphelandra where its cultural requirements will be met. Once it loses lower leaves, an inevitability you should accept at the outset, you may wish to place a smaller plant in front of it to cover the bare lower stem. A small fern or philodendron will do the job perfectly.

Potting and Soil: When necessary, repot the aphelandra in a new container about 2 inches larger in diameter than the old one. Use a clay, plastic, or ceramic container. A mix of 2 parts packaged potting soil and 1 part perlite is suitable.

Pruning: Your aphelandra can be pruned by cutting back the stem or stems just above a leaf. This will force the plant to branch below where the cuts were made. Pruning results in a superior-looking specimen capable of bearing multiple flower stalks — one at each growing tip.

AVAILABILITY AND SELECTION

Buy a specimen with leaves down to the bottom of the stem. The foliage should be rich, green, and clearly marked. There should be no sign of mealybugs, a regular pest of aphelandra; check the point where the leaves join the stem as well as leaf undersides for these critters. Some plants are sold with a single stem; others have been pruned and are branched. The multistemmed specimens seem more dramatic, though this quality may increase their cost.

CHRYSANTHEMUMS

If a word-association test were given to an old-time plant lover, the clue "chrysanthemum" would surely elicit the response "autumn flower." Modern growers are more likely to say "a plant for all seasons," since mums, once available almost exclusively during fall — their natural blooming period — are now found in shops year-round.

If you are looking for a splashy plant with excellent indoor-keeping qualities, mums should fit the bill. There are several types available in a wide color range, so you are certain to find the perfect choice.

DESCRIPTION

The most prominent chrysanthemum feature is obviously *flower color*. The National Chrysanthemum Society, Inc., recognizes five color classes: white, yellow, purple-pink, bronze-orange, and red. Bicolored forms are also common. Flower and plant size vary, but most pot specimens are about 30 inches high and bear flowers 3 to 4 inches across.

The Society also groups mums by the *structure and arrangement of florets*. The four types most commonly grown in pots are decorative, single, spider, and anemone-flowered chrysanthemums. The decoratives constitute the overwhelming majority of pot plants. For the most part, when you see large stocks of potted mums for sale, particularly in supermarkets, they are decoratives. Their outer florets are longer than those in the middle and the "flower" is more or less flattened. Single mums are the up-and-coming type for pot culture. Their florets are arranged around a flattened disk of what are actually shorter florets. They closely resemble daisies and are, in fact, nicknamed "daisy mums." The dramatic and exotic spider mums are named for their long, thin, tubular florets. They are a bit more difficult to come by. Anemone mums are similar to singles but have longer disk florets and more closely resemble garden anemones.

CHRYSANTHEMUM

Mums are also grouped by the *method of pruning*, regardless of floral structure. On most pot mums, the plant's side shoots are removed, and only one flower is allowed to develop at the tip of each stem. This practice is called "disbudding" and results in fewer and larger flowers produced in a canopy above the foliage. Other pot mums are called "sprays." They are grown so that some or all of the lateral buds are allowed to develop, resulting in three to five smaller flowers per stem. It is easy to recognize which pruning method was used on your plant.

Finally, chrysanthemums are divided into two general groups based on *flowering dates*. There are garden mums, which have a natural blooming time from late August through September. In areas where the first frost is in early or mid-October, the plants bloom before the flowers can be damaged by below-freezing temperatures. There are also greenhouse mums, which bloom naturally from around late September through October. If planted outdoors, the flowers will certainly be killed should the first frost arrive during that time. Of course, exact blooming dates vary depending on the variety of chrysanthemum and the environmental conditions.

The distinction between garden and greenhouse mums is important if you intend to plant your mum outdoors in the spring. A greenhouse mum cannot be left outdoors in an area where the first frost comes in early October, or the flowers will be blackened by the cold. However, if the plant is only to be used for interior decoration until the flowers fade and is then discarded, this difference is of little consequence.

Selection

Before purchasing a chrysanthemum plant, give it the once-over. Check to see that there are healthy leaves down to the bottom of each stem. If lower leaves have become dry, there may be a foliage disease, microscopic plant parasites may be present, or there may have been a cultural error — probably overwatering. This condition may also indicate that the plant was grown in overcrowded conditions.

If you are buying plants off-season, carefully check the flowers for readiness. The blooms should be fully or almost fully opened. Buds that are just beginning to show color or are only partly opened may not develop fully indoors, though this seems to be less of a problem during the autumn.

Though most chrysanthemums found in the shops are trouble-free and picture-perfect, occasionally you will find a less-than-healthy specimen offered for sale. Mums attract a wide variety of pests. Aphids are a fairly common chrysanthemum visitor and can cause severe disfiguration if infestation is heavy; mealybugs, also quite prevalent, may be found at the point where a leaf joins the stem; spider mites are one of the worst chrysanthemum enemies and may infest both leaves and flowers; and whitefly, a true mum lover, can be detected by gently shaking the plant, causing these insects to take flight — you can't miss them.

Several diseases also affect mums, including powdery mildew, wilt, fungus leaf spot, stem rot, and flower blight. If you familiarize yourself with these maladies, their signs and symptoms can be easily detected and you will have no trouble avoiding the purchase of a sick plant.

Most chrysanthemums are not labeled, so you don't know if you are buying a garden mum or a greenhouse mum. Since this fact can be an important determinant of how you will handle and present the plant, try to find out from the shopkeeper which type he is selling. If he does not know (not an unusual occurrence), you should treat the plant as if it were a greenhouse type. Keep in mind, though, that garden mums are most often sold during the fall.

Cultural Requirements

Light: To keep flowers fresh for the longest period of time, keep newly acquired mums out of direct sun and provide bright filtered light for about 4 hours each day.

Temperature: Night temperatures of 45° to 55° F. and day temperatures below 68° F. will help prolong flower freshness and keep your display in top form for several weeks.

Moisture: Water potted mums thoroughly when the top layer of soil in the container feels dry to the touch. You may find that potted mums dry out more quickly between waterings than many other plants, so check them often.

Fertilizer: It is not necessary to fertilize chrysanthemums while they are in bloom. Plants have been kept on a rigorous fertilizing schedule by the grower who raised them, and they need no additional nutrients at this time.

Plant Care After Flowers Fade

Many people toss out the chrysanthemum after flowering as they would a bunch of cut flowers. For those who do not have outdoor gardens, this is sensible. But for those who have outdoor gardens, read on.

Planting Garden Mums Outdoors: After the chrysanthemum flowers fade, prune the plant back to half its size, place it on a windowsill that receives some direct sunlight, water thoroughly whenever the top soil layer feels dry, fertilize every month with a water-soluble chemical fertilizer high in phosphorus (such as a product with an analysis of 15-30-15), and maintain temperatures around 65° F.

After the last frost, most likely in mid-spring, the chrysanthemum can be planted outdoors. Mums should be planted in a sunny, well-drained spot where the soil has been enriched with organic matter such as peat moss or compost. They are a snap to grow, requiring little more than division every other spring and some slow-release, high-phosphorus, dry fertilizer *every* spring. A liquid feed applied every few weeks from spring through summer can be substituted for the dry fertilizer.

Early each summer prune mums to half their size — a practice that encourages a low bushy habit, helps avoid the need for staking, and prevents plants from coming into bloom too early. In winter, after the stems have died back, cut off the above-ground parts and cover the crown with a thick mulch of dry leaves, pine boughs, or wood chips for protection.

Planting Greenhouse Mums Outdoors: If you have a greenhouse mum, the care after flowering is the same as described for garden mums. The difference comes in spring when the mum is planted outdoors, if you live in an area where the first frost is in October or before. In that case, a different type of planting site must be selected. These plants tend to bloom from late September through October, after the first frost hits colder areas, and the flowers can be killed by low temperatures. If you can plant your mum in a protected area near the house or near a windbreak, the flowers may be spared any cold damage. If you live in a warmer part of the country, you'll have no problem, since the first autumn frost comes later than the flowering period of greenhouse chrysanthemums.

CACTI & OTHER SUCCULENTS

Cacti and other succulents are ideal for people who may not

CACTUS

always be around to water, fertilize, prune, or repot right on time. Make no mistake: succulents are not wholly neglectable; they are just more adaptable and less demanding of a rigorous schedule than most houseplants.

All succulents, including cacti, flower predictably if cared for properly. Many produce sensational blossoms, worthy rivals to any flowers you can name.

Many people use the terms "cactus" and "succulent" interchangeably. This is not correct. Succulent is the more general term and refers to plants that store water. Cacti comprise one family of succulents — there are many other succulents, but not all succulents are cacti. Cacti are generally leafless and store water in their stems. Other succulents store water in stems, leaves, and roots.

DESCRIPTIONS

Describing the succulents worth owning and giving would be a lifetime proposition. However, the following nine genera (groups of succulents) are frequently available, noted for their flowers, and worthy of a place in any collection. There are

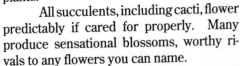

hundreds of other succulents just as wonderful, and their care is often identical to that required for these plants.

Aloe (Medicine Plant), Lily Family: These natives of Africa and Madagascar have been cultivated for centuries for their medicinal value, particularly the species *Aloe vera*. The jellylike sap that fills the fleshy leaves is used in many countries as a soothing ointment for cuts and burns; it is also used in many cosmetic preparations.

Aloe leaves are arranged in a rosette. The foliage of many species is toothed along the edges and is often beautifully marked with intricate patterns that look like they were painted on with a fine brush. Delicate flowers are produced abundantly along stalks growing from the center of the plant. Many varieties sucker freely; that is, they produce plantlets at the base of the mother *Aloe*, making propagation fast and easy.

Cereus (Night-Blooming Cereus), Cactus Family: Large tubular flowers of white, pink, or white and green are produced along the spine-ribbed stems of these South American natives. Most of these night-bloomers are upright-growing and free-branching. Since their flowers open at night and close by mid-morning, you may have to rise pretty early to catch the blossoms' full effect. It's worth it.

Crassula (Jade Plant), Crassula Family: There are about 300 species of *Crassula*, mostly native to southern Africa. The overwhelming favorite and the source of more questions than any other succulent is *Crassula argentea*, the jade plant. A well-grown specimen looks like a miniature tree or bonsai and can be a truly

ALOE

glorious pot plant. When planted outdoors, in parts of California and Florida, they bear an abundance of pink or white blossoms. Flowering indoors is rare and a cause for celebration.

Echeveria (Echeveria), Crassula Family: The echeverias are indigenous to Mexico and Central America. Those most commonly grown indoors produce ground-hugging rosettes of thick waxy leaves. They resemble succulent green roses. In mild climates echeverias are planted in rock or stone-wall gardens. Indoors they are exquisite in containers or mixed succulent arrangements. While all bear stalks of tiny flowers from the center of the plant, their most prominent features are their foliage form and texture.

Euphorbia (Crown-of-Thorns, Milk-Striped Euphorbia), Euphorbia Family:

67

The two *Euphorbia*s most commonly grown as houseplants are *Euphorbia splendens* (crown-of-thorns) and *Euphorbia lactea* (milk-striped euphorbia). The former bears gray-green heavily spined stems, oblong leaves about 1 inch long, and tiny flowers, which are normally pink-red, though yellow- and salmon-flowered varieties may be found. Plants generally reach about 4 feet in height. The crown-of-thorns may drop leaves at various times during the year, especially during winter. From late spring through summer new foliage develops to replace the foliage that was lost.

The milk-striped euphorbia is shaped like a candelabra. Its angular stems are marked with white and edged with stout spines. When cut, all *Euphorbia*s exude a white milky sap from leaves and stems, which causes a poison-ivy-like reaction or eye irritation upon contact. You must take great care in pruning and propagation.

Ferocactus (Barrel Cactus), Cactus Family: These natives of California, Texas, and Mexico are extremely popular with collectors. Barrel cactuses are usually densely clothed in colorful spines, which contrast beautifully with the large, bright-hued flowers borne at the tops of the plants. Most are rounded or oval, but they may also be cylindrical.

Lithops (Living Stones), Mesembryanthemum Family: There are approximately 40 species and 100 varieties of these southern African natives, all of which closely resemble highly polished stones — hence their common name. *Lithops* produce two thick semicircular leaves, flat on top, which grow to a diameter of about 3 inches. The leaves are separated by a narrow cleft from which new leaves grow, a pair at a time. The old pair of leaves withers and dies some time after the new pair is produced, and on it goes. Proportionately large white or yellow daisylike blossoms arise from the cleft.

Mammillaria (Pincushion Cactus), Cactus Family: There are over 150 species of *Mammillaria* hailing from Mexico and the United States. They are among the mainstays of the cactus garden because, unlike many cacti, they flower when young and are relatively easy to grow. Some produce a single, rounded stem, others cluster freely; some are covered with long white hairs, hooks, and stiff or soft spines. Plant color varies with species and variety. All *Mammillaria* have in common the absence of spined ribs and the presence of spine-tipped protuberances all over their stems, hence the nickname "pincushion." During the spring, *Mammillaria* produce a garland of white, yellow, pink, or magenta flowers, depending upon the variety, around the tops of the stems. Flowers are followed by long-lasting fleshy red fruits which some people claim are very tasty.

Selection

There are hundreds of succulents found in the trade, and the criteria that make each a specimen worthy of purchase are different. The best judgments are made only after examining the succulent collections in botanic gardens and nurseries and those of hobbyists who grow large groups of plants. Then you will be familiar with the qualities exhibited by well-grown specimens and will be able to spot a plant subjected to cultural malpractice from yards away. Until then, watch out for the following:

■ The stems of column-shaped cacti should be approximately the same diameter from top to bottom; they should not taper off or bulge out at any point, especially toward the tip — an indication that the plant has been grown under lower-than-optimum light levels or higher-than-recommended temperatures during one or more growing seasons.

■ Succulents should not require staking to stay upright unless they are extremely large. The need for staking may indicate that the root system is insufficient to support the plant, or that the plant has just been propagated and is not ready for sale.

■ Avoid buying succulents with soft, water-soaked, or brown areas on the stems — indications of a fungus or rot problem. Look especially closely at the point where the stem meets the soil line.

■ Branched succulents like jade plants should be stocky and compact, not sparse or thin-looking — indications of poor treatment, probably too little light.

■ The spines on new cactus growth are generally softer than those on older parts of the plant. Check to see if your plant has made recent growth or was neglected and did not grow at all during the last growing season.

■ Species that sucker freely, like aloes, should be potted in containers **large** enough to accommodate the mother plant and her **progeny**. Plants should not be hanging over the edge of the pot or be precariously situated in the container.

■ The foliage and stems of succulents should be plump and firm, not shrivelled or puckered — indications of a moisture problem, either too much or too little.

■ The spines on armored succulents should not be damaged, nor should the plant itself be seriously marred — indications of neglect or rough handling.

CULTURAL REQUIREMENTS

Light: The majority of succulents require at least 4 hours of direct sunlight each day. Place plants in front of the sunniest window in your home, preferably one that faces south, southeast, or east. The window should be unobstructed. Natural light is preferred, but if there is not a sunny window in your home, the existing sunlight can be supplemented with artificial light.

The best artificial light is fluorescent. A standard 4-foot fixture equipped with two 40-watt tubes — one cool white and one warm white — is ideal. A 4-foot, 4-tube fixture equipped with cool and warm tubes arranged alternately is even better. Set plants 6 to 12 inches from the light source if you are using only fluorescents. If the light fixture is a supplement to natural light, it can be placed higher above the plants.

Plants that are not getting enough light stretch out and become misshapen. This is especially true of cacti, whose stems decrease in diameter, permanently destroying their natural form. Other succulents may become so leggy that staking is required. Plants grown under lower than optimum light levels are also unlikely to flower. Succulents should be given a quarter turn every week or so to prevent them from

---

TIPS FOR PRUNING CACTUS

■ To prune a cactus that produces jointed pads, make a clean cut with a sharp knife at the joint.

■ The leaves of rosette-forming succulents like *Aloe* occasionally yellow and die. These leaves should be cut off close to the stem of the plant with a sharp knife. Breaking off the leaves of *Aloe* for use on minor cuts or burns does disfigure the plant, but if you use pieces of the older, lower leaves, it will not look as bad.

■ Shrublike succulents, such as the jade plant, should be pruned regularly by pinching the growing tips at a node— the point where a leaf joins the stem. This will encourage and promote fuller, more bushy growth. Jade plants are also pruned for purposes of shaping, sometimes to form a plant with a bare trunk and foliage at the top. This creates a treelike effect that is extremely attractive. Just cut the bottom growth off as close to the trunk as possible so that stubs are not left along the bare trunk.

leaning toward the light source.

Temperature: Most succulents grow best when temperatures from spring through fall are 60° to 65° F. at night and 5 to 15 degrees higher during the day; winter temperatures should be 45° to 55° F. at night, with daytime temperatures anywhere from 60° to 80° F. Cool winter nights are essential to initiate flower formation and to ensure a proper growth habit.

Moisture: When to water is the most frequently asked question about succulents, and improper watering results in the loss of more plants than any other factor.

Many growers achieve success by watering succulents other than cacti when the top *half* of soil in the container feels completely dry to the touch. Then water thoroughly. During winter you may find that the soil dries at a different rate than at other times of the year.

Cacti require less water than other pot plants, to be sure, but like all living things they require moisture to survive. The key is balance. Cacti in the home are generally killed by a *lack* of moisture rather than too much. This is the result of the popular notion that cacti do not need any water or water only

HANDLE WITH CARE

A spiny succulent is not a joy to repot, for obvious reasons. Protect yourself by putting on a pair of heavy rubber household gloves, then a pair of heavy-duty garden gloves, and work slowly and carefully. Always put the gloves in the washing machine to clean, because tiny cactus bristles become imbedded in the gloves. Other than the need to protect your hands, the principles of repotting succulents are the same as for any other plant.

in infinitesimal amounts. In the wild, cacti develop long roots that can absorb water from deep within the earth. Therefore, periods of drought, even when extended, find cacti thriving and flowering. In a container, the landscape is very different — the roots have nowhere to go in search of water, and regular replenishment is necessary.

Fertilizer: Every succulent fancier will give you different advice on when to fertilize and how much fertilizer to apply. One approach is the application of a high-phosphorus fertilizer, the water-soluble type, with an analysis of 15-30-15 at half strength every month from the time new growth appears in spring through midautumn. Withhold fertilizer for the rest of the year.

With other succulents, like aloes or jade plants, fertilize once a month with the same product. Apply the fertilizer at full strength from mid-March through mid-November.

Potting and Soil: A soil mix that works well for most succulents contains equal parts of packaged potting soil and a coarse grade of builder's sand — the type with little pieces of gravel scattered throughout. Depending on plant size, mix a teaspoon to a tablespoon of bonemeal into the volume of mix placed in the bottom half of the pot. Bonemeal is a slow-release organic fertilizer that supplements the water- soluble chemical product recommended above.

Cacti can often go 2 years between repottings, increasing pot size by ½ inch to 1 inch for big plants. Other succulents should be repotted when roots grow through the drainage holes, when the soil dries out more quickly than usual between waterings, when water runs through the soil faster than in the past, or when plants have made rapid growth since their last repotting. Select a new container ½ to 1 inch larger than the old one, depending on plant size. Also repot, regardless of other factors, when the potting soil has begun to feel and look compacted or muddy, which happens as it breaks down. If your plant needs fresh soil but does not require a larger container, you can remove some of the old medium from the top of the soil mass and replace it with fresh soil.

PAPERWHITES

Forcing Bulbs

Few gardening arts provide more satisfaction than forcing spring bulbs to bloom ahead of schedule. Defying Mother Nature's plan by providing extravagant blooms for your home is guaranteed to pull you out of the winter doldrums. You may reasonably wonder why flowers forced for winter bloom are discussed in this section. The explanation is twofold: The best bulbs are available in the fall, and that is when the forcing process begins.

Bulbs Requiring No Cold Treatment

Bulbs that cannot survive a northern winter outdoors are referred to as *tender bulbs*. Their need for warm temperatures makes them ideal for successful indoor cultivation. Many of the tender bulbs are conditioned by professional growers to flower ahead of their natural season. Your job is simply to provide a few basic cultural requirements, and — presto — a pot full of flowers.

There is, however, a slight hitch. Many of these bulbs, including the paperwhites, are a one-shot deal. The rigamarole they are put through by professionals to bloom early saps their strength, and all of their remaining energy is channeled into producing one, and only one, set of flowers.

Paperwhites: The small-flowered *Narcissus* varieties, or daffodils, all of which are known collectively as paperwhites, are the most commonly grown tender bulbs. Three readily available varieties are the Paperwhite (Polyanthus) *Narcissus,* with comparatively large, sweet-scented white flowers; the Soleil d'Or, with golden yellow flowers and a bright orange center "cup"; and the Chinese Sacred Lily, with white flowers and a bright yellow cup. Their cultural requirements are identical and simple.

The pebble method for growing paperwhites is an old standard. Its only drawback is that pebbles will not support wooden stakes should they be required to hold the stems upright as the plants prepare to bloom. You can substitute a mixture of 2 parts moistened peat moss and 1 part perlite for the pebbles. This mix will support stakes to which the stems can be inconspicuously tied with green twist ties. Bulbs planted in this mix should be cared for exactly as described for bulbs planted in pebbles.

Colchicums: Another bulb that does not require a cold period, though it is not tender or pretreated, is *Colchicum autumnale major.* Unfortunately, it is nicknamed "autumn crocus" — which it is not. Forcing *Colchicum* to bloom is a cinch. Just place the bulb on a windowsill. That's it. You don't need water, soil, or a pot. One *Colchicum* bulb (actually a bulblike structure called a corm) will produce a succession of blooms in lilac-pink, deep lilac, or lavender, depending on variety, atop stalks about 6 inches high. Flowers appear within a few weeks after the bulbs have been exposed to light and will last a week or more. After flowering, the bulb can be planted in a well-drained part of the garden, where it will bloom again the following fall. *Colchicum* make perfect "living gifts" for children, who are certain to be fascinated by their magical ability to bloom in very short order and without any assistance.

BULBS REQUIRING COLD TREATMENT

The "Dutch trio" of hardy bulbs — tulips, daffodils, and hyacinths — forces beautifully indoors. Varieties of all three reward indoor gardeners with displays from January though

April, as long as they receive a sufficient cold period — generally 10 to 14 weeks. Planting is most often done between October 1 and December 1. With staggered starting dates, you can have a steady supply of blooms for most of the winter.

Most growers agree that hyacinths are the easiest of the hardy bulbs to force. Medium-sized, trumpet-type daffodils recommended for forcing are in second place. Tulips are consid-

THE PEBBLE METHOD FOR FORCING PAPERWHITE NARCISSUS

- Find a shallow bowl, without drainage holes, about 4 inches deep.

- Pour pea gravel halfway to the top of the bowl. The gravel, available at garden centers and most hardware stores, serves to anchor the bulbs in place. Neither soil nor fertilizer is required.

- Set the bulbs, pointed-end up, side-by-side, on top of the gravel. Place as many bulbs as possible in the container; the fuller the pot, the more attractive the display. It doesn't matter if the bulbs are touching.

- Pour water into the bowl up to, but not quite touching, the base of the bulbs.

- Carefully surround the bulbs with more pebbles so they are held firmly in place. The bulbs should just poke up above the pebbles.

- Set the newly potted bulbs in a cool, dark spot, such as a basement or a cool closet, for about 3 weeks. During this time they will develop a root system sufficient to support the top growth that will be produced later.

- Check every week to see if the pebbles beneath the base of the bulbs are dry. If so, add water. Try to prevent the water from coming up to the bulbs — this could cause them to rot.

- After 3 weeks in a cool basement or closet, place the pot on a sunny windowsill. In about 6 to 8 weeks the bulbs will be in bloom. This period is the perfect time for giving. Assuming a mid-October start, blooms will appear in late January.

- Throughout the blooming period, continue to water when the pebbles beneath the base of the bulbs feel dry to the touch — and enjoy.

ered the most difficult for the novice, though double-flowering tulips (the multipetaled forms) do somewhat better than the singles. Regardless of which you choose, it is essential to select bulbs *recommended for forcing.* They should be labeled as such either in the plant catalog from which you are shopping or on the display stand at your garden center.

There are several ways to provide the 10 to 14 weeks of 35° to 45° F. temperatures required before these bulbs can be forced into bloom. The easiest way is to place the pots in an unheated cellar or garage where temperatures naturally fall within this range. Lower temperatures may cause the soil to freeze and the bulbs will be ruined. Higher temperatures will not satisfy the cold requirement

For apartment dwellers, the lowest shelf of your refrigerator might do, though this method is not always successful. Apartment dwellers with balconies could try placing potted bulbs in Styrofoam coolers covered with pine boughs and set against the building for protection against the cold.

Generally, hardy bulbs, like tender ones, can be forced for winter blooming only once. They are then discarded, unless you decide to plant them outdoors. If you do, cut off the flowers after they have faded, but leave the green flower stalks and foliage intact. Keep the pots on a sunny windowsill and continue to water when the top soil layer feels dry. The vegetative plant parts (the stalk and the leaves) produce the food to nourish next year's flowers and until they yellow naturally, should be cared for like any other foliage plant with regard to light and water. That is, they should be placed on a windowsill that receives some direct sunlight, watered when the top layer of soil in the container feels dry to the touch, and fertilized about once a month with a water-soluble chemical fertilizer recommended for use on houseplants. Given this treatment, the leaves will yellow and wither slowly and naturally.

When weather permits, unpot the bulbs and plant them outdoors in a well-drained site. Set the bulbs about 1 inch deeper than they were planted in the forcing container. The bulbs may be separated, but they seem to do best when they are unpotted and planted as a group — just as they were arranged in the container. Bulbs transferred outdoors should bloom the second spring after forcing and for several years to come.

AVAILABILITY AND SELECTION

Bulbs are available at florist and garden shops and through mail-order catalogs from early autumn through Christmas — or slightly beyond. Obviously, the earlier you start, the more ahead of season your bulbs will bloom.

When ordering bulbs by mail, you must, of course, trust your source. If you are hand-picking bulbs at the local garden center, look for large firm bulbs with no soft or rotten spots. Also, the *tunicate* (the onionskin-like shell that covers the bulb), which serves as protection for the bulbs, should be intact.

Tips for Planting Cold-Treated Bulbs

■ For planting, obtain what are known as bulb pans, either plastic or clay. They are available through well-supplied garden centers and plant shops. Bulb pans are shallower than standard-sized pots and offer a more pleasing balance between bulbs and container.

■ Place a clay shard or small piece of wire screen over the drainage hole in the bottom of the container to prevent soil loss.

■ Prepare a potting mixture of equal parts packaged potting soil, peat moss, and coarse sand or perlite.

■ Place bulbs of a single variety in one pot. Bulbs in a mixed planting are unlikely to bloom simultaneously and often produce an aesthetically confusing display.

■ Fill the pot about halfway to the top with the mix.

■ Set the bulbs, pointed-end up, on the soil surface — just far enough apart to prevent them from touching — and very gently twist them into place. Pot as many bulbs in the pan as will reasonably fit.

■ Fill the cracks between each bulb with mix and cover the bulbs so that just the tip of each is poking through the soil. The soil surface should be about ½ inch below the pot's rim to allow ample room for watering.

■ Soak thoroughly by pouring water just inside and all around the rim of the pot, not down through the middle of the bulbs.

■ Label each pot with the date planted, as well as the name and color of the bulbs.

■ Check weekly to see if moisture is required. If so, water thoroughly, until water runs through the drainage holes in the bottom of the container.

If you buy all your bulbs at the same time and do not have the opportunity to plant them right away, or you wish to stagger planting dates to get a succession of blooms, the unused bulbs can be stored for about 6 weeks. They should not be left hanging around carelessly, or they will soon dry out or rot, depending on moisture conditions. To maintain the bulbs properly, store them inside a perforated paper bag or net-type

FORCING COLD-TREATED BULBS

- During the cold-treatment period, check the pots regularly to see if moisture is required. If so, water thoroughly.

- When 2 inches of growth has appeared, place the pots in a room at about 60° F., out of direct sunlight, for about 2 weeks, just until the growing tips turn green. Since the tips have developed in the dark, they will start out white.

- Force bulbs into bloom by placing the pots on a sunny windowsill in a room where temperatures are 65° to 70° F. Higher temperatures may result in growth that is weak and floppy.

- Continue to water whenever the top layer of potting mix feels very dry to the touch.

- Staking may be required to hold the leaves and flower stalks upright. Thin green bamboo stakes (available at garden centers) and green twist ties work beautifully for this purpose.

potato sack in a dry, cool, dark, well-ventilated spot. Never use plastic. If such a place does not exist, the vegetable crisper in your refrigerator will suffice. Avoid storing bulbs in the light, which may cause them to start growing prematurely.

GROWING ACCESSORIES

Hyacinth Glasses: Hyacinth glasses are special vases, usually glass, designed for growing hyacinths in water without using any soil.

The vases are designed so that the bulbs rest on a bowl-shaped ledge at the top and roots grow down through the neck of the container into a flared base. The base is filled with water, and the bottom of the bulb sits ever so slightly above the water. Every few weeks the vase must be checked to see if water needs to be added or if it requires changing. A few pieces of charcoal placed in the bottom of the bulb glass will help keep the water fresh.

Place the bulb glass in a cool basement or in your refrigerator until a heavy mass of roots fills the base and there is 2 to 3 inches of top growth. This will take about 8 to 12 weeks. Then gradually bring the vase into the sunlight of a bright windowsill.

There are a number of hyacinth varieties recommended for this treatment, and you should stick with them for best results. There are also crocus vases, which are a smaller version of the hyacinth glass. They are used for giant-flowered crocus varieties, which are treated exactly like hyacinths.

Crocus Bowls: Special crocus planters are also offered in shops and through mail-order companies. The most popular types are more delicate versions of the traditional strawberry jar, usually made of delft, in the Dutch tradition. These bowls have a wide opening at the top and several smaller openings scattered along the sides of the planter. The crocuses are planted so that they gracefully slip through all the openings in the jar as they grow, creating a very pleasant effect. The bowls are generally sold with the appropriate quantity of growing medium, the bulbs themselves, and instructions for planting and forcing the crocuses into flower. The crocuses used in these kits generally bloom 6 to 7 weeks after planting — a shorter period than that required by the Dutch trio. The same type of bowl is also sold with white or blue scillas (also known as wood hyacinths) substituted for the crocuses.

INDEX